HOSTAGE IN THE WOODS

By Cynthia Wall, KA7ITT

**Published by the
American Radio Relay League
Newington, CT USA 06111**

Cover art by Sheila Dianne Somerville

For Lenore
W6NAZ
With Admiration

CONTENTS

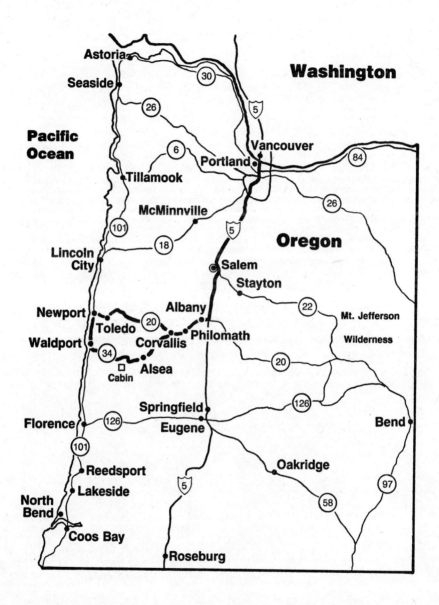

Chapter 1

On the Road Home

Friday, December 19th — 3 p.m.
Near Corvallis, Oregon

"I t's snowing!" Kim exclaimed happily as Marc turned on the windshield wipers to sweep away the sudden flurry of crystalline flakes swirling onto the windshield.

"Perfect," said Kim, leaning over to kiss Marc lightly on the cheek. "The last day of fall term, Christmas is coming . . ."

"And I finally have a chance to be with you," interrupted Marc impatiently. "Where have you been the last two weeks, anyway? Every time I've called the dorm, you've been out."

"Zoology lab, chemistry lab, calculus, my job in the biology lab," Kim counted the reasons off on her fingers, amused by Marc's look of disappointment. "And by the way," she added, "where have *you* been when *I* called?"

"Physics lab, finishing my Pascal program, setting up the new twenty-meter antenna for the Amateur Radio Club . . .," Marc recited, starting to smile a little.

"Say no more," Kim laughed. "We're both just incredibly busy people. But I'm glad you offered to take me and all my stuff home."

Marc started to reply but suddenly focused on the rear view mirror.

"Hang on!" he shouted to Kim as he pulled his '78 Chevy Malibu sharply over to the shoulder of the road. The rear end of the car fishtailed on the snow-coated gravel shoulder. Marc carefully turned the wheels into the skid to avoid spinning 360 degrees on the narrow road. They came to a bumpy stop, straddling some tall roadside grass.

"What on earth?" Kim exclaimed as a brown van hurtled past them on the road, barely missing the rear end of their car. She and Marc watched in amazement as the van slid back and forth on the road, almost out of control, and then disappeared around a bend in the road in a cloud of snow spray and exhaust.

"Are you okay?" Marc turned to Kim.

"Yes, I'm fine," she said, shuddering slightly. "Good thing we've got things packed in here so tight," she said, surveying their piles of books and clothes in the back seat. "I wonder what their hurry was?"

"Me too," said Marc, reaching over to turn on his two-meter "ham radio" mounted under the dash. He and Kim sat quietly, catching their breath from the sudden stop as Marc punched up first the Corvallis and then the Salem area Amateur Radio repeater frequencies. "Repeater" stations, at higher locations, retransmitted and spread signals over a wide area. Kim was always impressed with how her radio's one or two watts could be rebroadcast from a repeater and heard almost one hundred miles away. Marc shrugged his shoulders as both frequencies came up quiet.

"I guess we're the only hams to have seen those clowns," Marc said. "I'm tempted to call the police and report that van, but I guess it wasn't really an emergency."

"It will be if they keep driving like that," Kim added grimly.

Marc pulled the car carefully back out on the road and drove slowly, whistling at the skidding tire tracks the van made going around the corner in the wet snow.

"Now where were we?" he asked Kim.

"Seeing who could list the most excuses why we haven't seen each other this month," said Kim.

"Oh yes," said Marc, lowering his voice dramatically. "Kim, the fair maiden of the airwaves who saved my life just a mere seven months ago* has given up all romance in the pursuit of academic excellence. While she tries to capture the

*See Night Signals, published 1989 by ARRL.

Nobel Prize in veterinary medicine, poor Marc dies of a broken heart. And here I am, just barely recovered from a broken leg." He added a little dramatic sob at the end which made Kim laugh and poke him in the ribs.

"Your leg's been well since August," laughed Kim. "If I had known you were going to feel sorry for yourself, maybe I should have left you in the snow," she said, teasing, but giving him another kiss which implied more than her words, how she really felt. "And by the way, just for the record, I'm not sure I'm majoring in vet medicine It might be marine biology or pre-med. After all, I *am* just a freshman."

"Well all right," said Marc, still with his stage voice. "I forgive you."

"For being a freshman? Or not knowing my major? And did I ask to be forgiven?" retorted Kim, laughing.

"No," Marc said, trying to keep a straight face. "But I forgive you anyway."

They settled into the easy conversation that had deepened their friendship since their dramatic meeting the previous May. Soon they were discussing plans for the holidays. Marc lived in Portland, an hour north of Kim's home in Salem, but they could meet for shopping, ice skating, and movies. Kim stretched luxuriously at the thought of free time for fun. She hadn't told Marc yet that she would be spending three days at her aunt's house in Portland while she volunteered at a special project at Mercy Hospital. Maybe she and Marc would be able to meet for dinner one or two of those nights.

"KA7SJP to KA7ITR," she teased, reciting their respective Amateur Radio call letters just as they did at the beginning of their radio transmissions to each other. "Permission to turn off the ham radio and find some mood music?"

"KA7SJP from KA7ITR — permission granted," Marc laughed as he dialed the car radio to Kim's favorite soft jazz station.

The snow flurries were letting up, and for a few miles, the sun broke through the clouds, making the snow-dusted roadways and fields glisten in winter light.

Kim leaned back against the headrest and closed her eyes. She was tired. Her first term at Oregon State University in Corvallis had been more rewarding than she had anticipated. It had also been more work. She smiled as she thought with satisfaction of the final exams she had just completed. She felt confident her grades would be good. She wished she knew for sure what her major was going to be, but perhaps this Christmas vacation would help her to decide.

She looked over at Marc who was concentrating on the road. He reached up and pushed a lock of his wavy brown hair off his forehead. She thought back to that lonesome night after the senior prom when she had first talked to him by Morse code on Amateur Radio. *And to think I thought he was probably ugly,* she mused to herself. *Handsome, intelligent, fun . . . he was all of those things.* She had never dreamed Amateur Radio would lead her to romance.

Her daydreams were cut short by a bulletin on the radio.

"The Corvallis National Bank was held up a half hour ago by three men believed to be part of 'The Valley Gang' responsible for more than ten robberies this month in the Willamette Valley. One of the suspects, William Steimer, was seriously wounded in the robbery attempt. He has been airlifted to the trauma center at Mercy Hospital in Portland. The other two suspects are believed to be Bernie Knissen, a Caucasian male with black curly hair, approximately six feet tall and one hundred eighty pounds and Joe Steimer, also a Caucasian male, five foot ten with brown hair. They were last seen escaping in a brown, older-model Dodge van, believed to be driven by a blonde woman who may also have been wounded by police. In the exchange of gunfire, a Corvallis police officer was also injured. The suspects are considered to be armed and dangerous. Anyone seeing a van or suspects answering this description is asked to call the Benton County Sheriff's Office or Corvallis Police."

Kim and Marc looked at each other in astonishment.

"That was them! Did you see the license number?" Kim asked.

"K — something, I think," said Marc, "but I'm not sure."

Kim had already turned off the radio and was tuning the two-meter radio to the Corvallis repeater. Two men, Eric Reed, N7NSG, and Cliff Siddell, N7FLE, were talking. Marc's face brightened when he heard the call letters N7FLE.

"Good, that's Cliff — he's got a phone patch" (way of connecting a phone line to Amateur Radio), Marc said. "Break, break." Marc said the words indicating an emergency situation in the split second between the men's transmissions. Cliff came back.

"Go ahead break."

"N7FLE this is KA7ITR — Cliff, could you phone to the sheriff's office in Corvallis."

"I'll do better than that," Cliff replied. "I have a new phone patch — stand by a minute and you can talk directly to the sheriff's office yourself."

"Benton County Sheriff's Office. Dispatch."

"Hello, my name is Marc Lawrence. I'm an Amateur Radio operator traveling east on Highway 34. I believe we were just passed by the brown van wanted in the Corvallis bank robbery."

The dispatcher got the details of his exact location and then took his home phone number down for further reference.

Kim and Marc drove along, watching intently for any signs of the brown van. One Oregon State Police car passed them at high speed, not to be seen again. South of Albany, Marc's Chevy turned left onto I-5 and headed north toward Salem.

"So, we've been run off the road by the infamous Valley Gang," said Marc.

Kim laughed. The "Valley Gang" had gained notoriety in the news the last month for several successful and attempted robberies. They had become sort of a joke in the local papers as reports indicated that their takes at various banks had been very low. On one robbery in Albany, the bag of money, also containing some marked bills coated with explosive marker dye, had actually detonated in the hands of one of the robbers leaving the bank. A cartoon drawing of him with bright red hands and pants made the front page of the paper the next morning.

"We've been joking about them, but there's sure nothing funny about shooting at people," said Kim.

"No," agreed Marc.

They were pulling into the outskirts of Salem. The snow had stopped falling and the dusting on the ground was quickly turning to slush. Marc reached over and touched Kim on the shoulder.

"So let's make some real plans for vacation, Kim. I promised my dad I'd help him with some projects this weekend, but I could meet you Monday — either in Portland or Salem," Marc said.

Kim drew a deep breath.

"Now don't get mad, Marc, but actually I'm going to be in Portland on Monday — in fact Monday through Christmas Eve on Wednesday night. Do you remember June Blakely WA6OPS — the one who's the Recreational Therapy Director at Mercy Hospital?"

Marc nodded yes, his face one big question mark.

"Well," Kim continued, "she's staging a big North Pole Network this year where the kids talk to Santa via Amateur Radio. She called me a couple of weeks ago and asked if I would help. When I told her I was still considering a possible career in medicine, she suggested I come up and volunteer for a few days — I still have my Candystriper uniform from my junior volunteer work, and she said she could arrange it for me to work in several departments."

Marc was silent; his face showed his disappointment.

"Oh come on, Marc," Kim pleaded. "Look, I tell you what. Will you help me with the kids on Christmas Eve? We have both Santas that we need all arranged, but we still need several more hams to help with the kids so they can talk to the North Pole. And," she said, her voice speeding up, "we can go out to dinner afterwards — I'm going to be staying at my aunt's right near the hospital. And we'll be together on Christmas Eve."

Marc was still frowning.

"Mercy Hospital," he said quietly. "Isn't that where the radio just said they had taken the wounded bank robber?"

"Yes, I think it was. Well, maybe he can play the Grinch," Kim said lightly.

She looked over at Marc and added, "Unless you want that role?"

They had just pulled into her driveway. Marc laughed in spite of his disappointment.

"Oh Kim, I just want to spend some time with you — that's all. Okay, you win. I'll be lead elf or Rudolph or whatever you want me to be on Christmas Eve if you'll promise to save some time for me the following week."

"I promise," Kim said. "I really do."

They kissed softly, and Marc held her close for a moment. Being with this whirlwind of a girl was certainly never dull. He sighed and grabbed her heavy stack of books to carry into the house.

Chapter 2

"Wanted"

Friday, December 19th, 3:15 p.m.
Between Corvallis and Interstate 5.

"Can you drive this thing or not?" Bernie shouted. "I'm trying," Sheila yelled back as the brown van lurched back and forth on the slippery road. "It's not so easy with one arm, you know!"

"There — go down there," said Joe, pointing at a narrow dirt road leading to a grove of trees.

Sheila swerved and cursed as the van bounced over the rutted road.

"Oh, my arm," she groaned, holding her blood-soaked left elbow. Joe reached over and grabbed the steering wheel to make the sharp turn in between the tall fir trees. With Sheila pressing lightly on the gas pedal and Joe holding the wheel, they managed to maneuver the van in behind a large clump of evergreen blackberry vines.

Joe jumped out on the passenger side and looked back at the main highway anxiously.

"I think we're hidden."

"I suppose we're going to camp here?" Bernie asked sarcastically, shivering slightly as the winter air poured in the open door. "The infamous Valley Gang takes cover in the blackberry bushes," he sneered.

"That's exactly what we're going to do until it's dark," said Joe. "Probably every cop in the state is looking for us now. Our only chance is to wait until night, get another car, and then find a place to hole up."

"Let's just go back to the cabin — why'd we come this way anyway?" grumbled Bernie. "The cabin is west of here."

Joe shook his head in disbelief.

"You'd think for all the time you spent in the slammer, you'd know that you don't lead the cops right back to where you live."

Sheila moaned slightly.

"It's all your fault," she said accusingly to Joe and Bernie. "How many holdups in one month and what have we got to show for it? A bunch of large bills which are probably marked, me wounded, Willy probably dead, and if you killed that guard, a murder rap waiting for all of us."

The two men were silent. Bernie lit a cigarette and stared at the floor. This certainly wasn't what he had bargained for when he had agreed to join up with Joe six weeks ago. The two of them had been cellmates for a year in a Northern California prison — Bernie serving twenty years for armed robbery and Joe three years for a lesser robbery charge. Before Joe was released on parole, the two of them had made plans for Joe to help Bernie escape from the work detail that often cleared weeds on the highway nearby.

The escape had gone as planned. Joe and Bernie drove a stolen car to Medford, Oregon, where they joined up with Sheila, Joe's longtime girlfriend, who had been working as a waitress until Joe jumped parole. Now as she began to moan again and complain to Joe, Bernie turned to her angrily.

"Shut up!" he ordered. "It can't be that bad. All you do is complain anyway. To hear Joe talk about you in prison, you were some sort of angel — he never told me that he had a dumb whiner for a girlfriend."

Joe grabbed Bernie by the collar and shoved him hard away from the van's door.

"Cool it, just cool it — both of you," Joe said. "Now we're going to stay here until dark and then we're going to get another car somewhere . . ."

"And head south to San Diego — where you worked that summer on a fishing boat, right?" Sheila pleaded.

"San Diego?" Joe asked. "We're not going to San Diego or anywhere until we get Willy out of that Portland Hospital. I'm not leaving my kid brother behind and that's final!"

Bernie ground his cigarette out in the snow and stomped off down the road.

* * * * * * * * * * * * * * * * * *

Monday, December 22nd
In a rundown motel on the edge of Portland.

"The Corvallis Bank robbery suspect continues in critical condition at Mercy Hospital. Portland authorities are hoping that by the end of the week he will be able to be questioned about the robbery and other members of the alleged 'Valley Gang.' The police officer shot during the holdup attempt has been upgraded to good and may be released by Christmas. Meanwhile, police have located the brown van believed to have been used in the robbery. The van was abandoned in an alley near Albany."

Joe switched off the television and began pacing in the small, dingy motel room.

"What are you scratching at?" he questioned Bernie who was sitting with one pant leg rolled up. He was vigorously scratching the reddened skin on his shin.

"I don't know," Bernie said angrily. "Hey, what's this?" he asked, plucking a red leaf from his sock.

Sheila burst out laughing.

"Leaves of three — let it be!" she howled with laughter. "That's poison oak, you dummy. Don't you know anything?" she said to Bernie who dropped the leaf like a hot potato.

"You had better go take a shower and wash that stuff off," Joe said quietly.

Sheila stopped laughing and turned her attention back to herself.

"I'm hungry," she complained.

"Here," Bernie said, tossing her a bag of potato chips on his way to the bathroom.

"No more chips — I'm sick of chips. How about some Chinese food or Mexican food? Remember when we used to go out to the Green Lantern and have chow mein, Joe?"

Joe raised his head from the half-slumbering position he had assumed in the only chair in the room.

"What?" he asked Sheila.

"I said," she repeated, her voice rising to a high whine, "do you remember the Green Lantern there in Yreka where we used to go? That was a long time ago — before you got caught robbing that liquor store," she said wistfully. "Remember how we used to break open our fortune cookies and you'd say, 'You're all the fortune I need, Baby!'"

"Shut up, Sheila." Joe said. "I'll go get us some food."

"Chinese, okay? Or maybe some tacos or something," Sheila suggested hopefully as Joe slipped out the motel door into the dark night.

Bernie glared at her.

"I don't know why I hang around with you — you're all a bunch of losers," Bernie said, his voice surly with anger.

"You don't, huh?" Sheila said. "Well, I'll tell you why. Because Joe is smarter than you'll ever be. Because he's the one who knew about his cousin's cabin on the river, because he's the one who got you out of jail —that's why. And he's the one that will get us out of this mess."

Bernie pounded one fist into the other and then slowly lit a cigarette. Sheila's whining voice made him want to wring her neck, but his fear of Joe kept him in control. And unfortunately, what Sheila had just said was true. He was alone, without connections. Right now, he had to stick with Joe, but maybe later . . .

He watched television for the next half hour, trying to ignore Sheila. Just when Bernie thought he couldn't stand her complaints any longer, Joe came back in the door, his arms loaded with fast food sacks.

"Tacos all around," he announced cheerfully.

"Anyone see you?" Bernie asked.

"Of course they saw me, stupid. But I don't think anyone's going to notice a guy standing in a fast food line. In fact, I think that's a lot safer than going into a market where there are newspapers with drawings of us all over the place."

"Just the same, I don't like it," Bernie said. "We need to get out of here and do it soon."

"Look," Joe answered. "That's exactly what they'd expect us to do. I bet they've got Interstate-5 covered like hawks. We're better off just staying in the area for awhile."

"You really think that, Joe?" Bernie asked sarcastically. "Even with your brother in the hospital? You don't think they aren't expecting you to come back for him? And you're always calling me stupid!"

"Sure are good tacos, Joe!" Sheila said with her mouth full.

* * * * * * * * * * * * * * * * * * *

Tuesday, December 23rd, 6 p.m.

"Does that feel better, Baby?" Joe asked almost tenderly as he rebandaged Sheila's arm with strips from a pillowcase.

"It aches all the way up to my shoulder," said Sheila with tears in her eyes.

"I'm sorry, Sheila, really I am. But I don't think there's any bullet in it — looks like it just kind of went through the flesh above your elbow and came out the other side. After we get Willy, we'll head for California. Once we get across the border, we'll get some help for both you and Willy."

"Ain't you been listening to the news?" said Bernie.

"They've said 'critical condition' about your brother. You'll be lucky if he lives to the border."

"Not Willy. He's tough," said Joe. "I bet it's not as bad as they say, anyway. But Sheila can check all that out tonight."

"Oh Joe, please don't make me go to the hospital," pleaded Sheila.

"It's our only way, Baby. We've got to find out where Willy is for tomorrow night. We can't just be wandering around in the halls looking for him."

"But supposing I get caught?" whined Sheila.

"You won't if you do what I told you. Now here's a raincoat I bought at a store down the street. With the Christmas crowds, nobody paid any attention to me. You just put this coat on around your shoulders so it will cover up your bandaged arm. Carry this box of candy in your right hand and you'll look just like any other visitor."

"Tell me again what I do when I get there, Joe. I don't remember so good," said Sheila, drying her tears.

"Well, you walk past the information desk," Joe began patiently, "but if they stop you, tell them you know where you're going. And if they ask for a specific name, say 'Mary Seville'— the paper here says she was hurt in a car wreck and was airlifted to Mercy Hospital."

"Be our luck that she's dead, now," Bernie growled.

"Name isn't in the obits today," said Joe. "I checked.

"So anyway, you get on the elevator and go to the fifth floor. I think that's where he'll be. I called the hospital operator and found out that's where intensive care is and also patients just out of there. So you look for a guard standing in the hallway. I bet there'll be one and if you see one, you just stroll on down the hall and kind of peek in the room, if you can."

"What if the door's closed?" asked Sheila.

"Well then you don't peek," said Joe as if explaining something to a young child. "And don't go talking to the guard or walk so slow he gets a good look at you although nobody should know what you look like. And if you can't find him on that floor, just turn around and take the elevator or the stairs to sixth —he's got to be on one of those two."

"I don't know, Joe — sounds pretty risky to me," said Sheila.

"Do it for me, okay, Baby?" Joe asked and Sheila nodded unhappily.

"Now, can you do something to your hair?" Joe asked.

"What about my hair?" Sheila said angrily. "You know I haven't exactly been able to go to a beauty parlor!"

She ran her fingers through her stiff bleached-blonde hair. Joe handed her his comb.

"Oh, all right! And I'll put on makeup, too," Sheila said as she marched into the bathroom carrying her purse.

When she appeared a few minutes later, she looked almost attractive. Joe helped her on with her coat, handed her

14

the candy, and walked out the door with her to the dark-blue stolen Chevy van in the parking lot.

"You'll be lucky if the cops don't pick you up with that car," said Bernie as they closed the door behind them.

"Yeah, what about that?" Sheila asked, her voice once again anxious.

"We're going to take back streets and we won't be out long — just have to risk it," Joe said.

They drove slowly through alleyways and side streets and soon came to the hospital, its ten floors of windows lit up in the evening darkness. Joe dropped Sheila off near the front door and told her he would park in an alley for twenty minutes and then be back.

* * * * * * * * * * * * * * * * * * *

Tuesday, December 23rd 7:30 p.m.

Sheila slid quickly into the passenger side of the van.

"Did you find him?" Joe asked as he drove the car around the corner and down a dark side street behind the hospital.

"Yeah, I found him — on the fifth floor, just like you said, Joe."

"Well?" Joe asked.

"Well what?" Sheila mimicked, trying to unwrap the box of candy with her right hand.

Joe grabbed it and tossed it on the floor. Sheila started to cry and Joe ignored her tears.

"Was there a guard? Did you see Willy?" he demanded of her.

"Yeah, there was a guard," sniffled Sheila, "but he didn't seem to be paying much attention to anyone. He was sitting on a chair against the wall, just reading a magazine. The door to Willy's room was closed, but just as I got up there near it, a nurse walked in and left it open behind her.

"There was a drinking fountain right there opposite the door — wasn't that lucky, Joe?" she asked waiting for his praise.

"Yeah, Baby, that was lucky. So then what happened?"

"Well, I stopped and took a long drink and then just kind of looked over my shoulder like this." Sheila turned her head and looked back over the van seat. "And then I saw Willy."

"Did he see you?"

"Naw, I doubt he saw nothing. Joe, he's all hooked up to tubes and machines and stuff and his eyes are closed like he's dead."

They drove on in silence to the motel parking lot.

"Thanks for going, Baby," Joe said as he pulled the key from the ignition.

"Can I have some of that candy now, Joe?" Sheila asked.

"Sure you can, Baby, sure you can," Joe said, unwrapping it for her.

* * * * * * * * * * * * * * * * * *

Wednesday, December 24th 11 a.m.

Sheila was getting tired of being questioned by Bernie.

"Look, I told all that stuff to Joe about how Willy looked," she said.

"Well tell me too, since I have to be part of this, okay?" Bernie urged, just barely keeping the anger in his voice under control.

Joe lay on the bed, quietly listening to them both. "Tell me more about the guard," Bernie demanded. "Did he have a gun?"

"Yeah, a big pistol right on his hip," Sheila said.

"Did you see Willy's legs?" Bernie asked.

"Why do you care about his legs?" Joe interrupted. "He wasn't hit in the legs."

"I want to know if they have leg irons on him, that's why," Bernie said quietly. "I was in the hospital once and they put leg irons on me — guard said they always did."

Sheila sat thinking.

"There was something metal around the end of the bed on one side, but I didn't see his legs — he was all covered up," Sheila said.

"So what do we do if he's in irons?" Joe asked.

"Key is probably on the guard — we'll just get it off him — or I might have something here that will work," Bernie said, fishing through his wallet. He produced a small metal key. "A buddy gave me this — always kept it."

"One size fits all?" Joe questioned.

"Maybe," Bernie said.

Suddenly, Sheila burst out laughing.

"So what's so funny?" Bernie growled.

"I was just thinking of you coming out of that bank in Albany when that bag of money blew up all over you," Sheila gasped, holding her sides with laughter.

"Yeah, well you wouldn't have thought it was so funny if you'd had that red powder all over your legs! Couldn't wash it off either," Bernie said. "To say nothing of all the money we lost. That bag was full, and it blew up all over the sidewalk."

"How'd they do that, anyway, Joe?" Sheila asked, still giggling.

"Oh, it's a special powder they put on the bills — explodes when it's jostled," Joe said.

"How much money we got left, Joe?" Sheila asked.

"About five thousand that we can use," Joe said.

Bernie sighed and began pacing again.

"So let's get Willy out and get going," he said, turning to Joe.

"Not until tonight," Joe insisted. "Christmas Eve ought to be a real quiet time in the hospital. Nobody wants to be out visiting sick people, then. We'll leave here at 7:30."

"Christmas Eve," Sheila said wistfully. "I wish I was home."

Joe ignored her. He started going over the plans once again.

"Sheila will let us off by the front door. Then she can drive around the block a few times and then park by the back door where I picked her up last night. Once we get Willy, we'll run for that entrance. I'll carry him, and you can cover me, Bernie."

"And then what, Joe? Then what?" Bernie demanded.

"Well, then we see how bad Willy is. If he's okay to travel, we'll head straight for the California border. If he's not — well then, I guess we'll go back to the cabin for a few days until he's feeling better."

Bernie shook his head in disgust. He lit his twentieth cigarette of the evening, scratched his leg, and began pacing in the small room.

Chapter 3

"North Pole Network"

December 24th — 6 p.m.
Mercy Hospital

Kim adjusted the red and green garlands around the window and turned to admire the twinkling lights on the Christmas tree in the middle of the fourth-floor pediatric ward playroom. Everything was set for "North Pole Network" due to start in just one half hour.

Some of the chairs had been moved to the edge of the room to allow space for those children who had to be brought in their beds. Marc had been around most of the afternoon helping to set up a base station in the middle of the playroom.

Children would gather around the transmitter, now to be connected by a coax cable to an antenna by the window. The black hand-held microphone was waiting for their first transmissions to Santa.

Santa, of course, was Ben Kingman, K6DKA, a longtime ham in the Portland area who enjoyed his annual role of Saint Nicholas. A grandfather himself, he was a natural for the part, with his booming laugh and gentle voice.

"How are you coming?" asked June Blakely, WA6OPS. She like Ben, was a transplanted Californian — now Recreational Therapy Director for Mercy Hospital. She whistled in admiration at the decorations. "Looks great, you two."

"I think we're all set," said Marc, adjusting the volume and running a practice check with Ben.

"Both Santas are close to the hospital, so we'll be able to use direct simplex frequencies. Kim and I each have handhelds and with two more volunteer hams coming shortly, we should have someone free to go to the rooms of the kids who can't be moved."

"Good — sounds like you've thought of everything," June said approvingly.

"Even an extra battery pack," said Kim smiling, holding a clip-on battery pack for her small, slender handheld Kenwood TH-25 two-meter radio. Her Uncle Steve, W6RHM, who had originally gotten her interested in ham radio, had given her this new transceiver after her dramatic adventure last spring. She admired it for a minute before slipping the pack and the transceiver into the deep pocket of her red and white Candystriper uniform.

"I see you changed from the green gown you were wearing in the nursery back to your old favorite," June said.

"Yes, it seems like it goes with the occasion," Kim said, running her finger down one of the red stripes of her skirt. "Besides, this uniform brings back a lot of happy memories."

"Is that the voice of a future doctor I hear?" Marc asked.

"Oh, I don't know," Kim said in frustration. "This has been a great three days — I've been so excited that the time has just flown by — I worked in ER, in orthopedics, in the nursery, but best of all here in pediatrics."

"That's the same tone in your voice that you had after volunteering in the vet-medicine lab last August," Marc said, laughing.

Kim nodded in agreement. "Why do people have to decide on being just one thing — I can think of twenty possibilities!"

June smiled. "Well you don't have to decide tonight. We've certainly appreciated having you here this week, Kim. You've done a great job." Noticing Kim's blush, she changed the subject. "I've got to attend to some last minute things, but I'll be back before the action starts. Our Candystriper junior volunteers are meeting down in the lounge in twenty minutes to help wheel all the kids in."

Kim watched June walk down the hall at her brisk, almost trot-like gait.

"She's a wonder," Kim said in admiration. "You can't believe how great she is with the kids. Adults too. She uses

20

Amateur Radio as therapy for people recovering from all sorts of illnesses. She has 'radio time' in therapy and patients are brought down to listen. Sometimes, stroke patients get so excited, wanting to talk back to the radio, that they utter their first words. And last year, there was a seriously ill young boy who had not eaten much in a week. After he talked to Santa, he began eating again. With June's charm and talent, I wouldn't be surprised if every patient dismissed from this hospital came out with a ham ticket!"

Marc laughed and then pulled Kim close.

"I missed you," he whispered.

"I missed you, too," Kim said, "when I had time," she added laughing. Then seeing his raised eyebrows, she added, "Seriously, I did miss you, but I've scarcely had time to think the last three days. I'll tell you all about it at dinner tonight after the party."

"Okay," he said, "promise?"

"I promise," she said, kissing him lightly.

"Oooh, look at Kim!" called a little boy from the doorway.

Kim and Marc parted, suddenly embarrassed.

"Hi, Jonathan," Kim called to him. "Come on in and help us get set to talk to Santa."

The red-haired seven-year-old boy grinned at Kim. His look was one of "okay — if you believe in Santa, I won't be the one to tell you." He came over and stood shyly beside Marc.

"Hi Tiger," Marc greeted him. "Want to help run these wires over to the wall for me?"

Jonathan was soon down on all fours in his blue pajamas, helping to tape wires down to the floor so no one would trip on them. When he came back to Kim, she put an arm around him easily.

"Jonathan's been my helper this week — he knows everyone and everything," Kim said as Jonathan beamed with pride. "Are you going home tomorrow?" she asked him.

"Yeah, for the day — as soon as I have my treatment," he said. "Doctor said I couldn't miss even one day."

"Leukemia," Kim whispered to Marc as Jonathan scampered to the doorway to greet the kids being wheeled in.

"They just started treatment two days ago. All that beautiful red hair will start falling out pretty soon."

Marc shook his head in sadness. But there was no time to feel sorry about the plight of children spending Christmas Eve in the hospital. Volunteers and kids poured into the lounge. A few walked, but most came in wheelchairs or beds. There was excited talking and giggling. Kim helped arrange the kids in a circle around the transmitter.

June was in and out of the room, bringing more volunteers and various supplies. All of the kids seemed to know her, and she managed to give several quick hugs on her trips back and forth.

"K6DKA, this is KA7ITR," said Marc. "Do you have Santa on the line?"

The kids' voices fell to a quiet hush as they listened to Marc establishing communications with Santa. Back of Santa's voice, they could hear static and wind-like noises. Kim smiled. What the children didn't realize was that the North Pole wind noises were from a tape Ben was playing. Ben Kingman, a well-known actor and opera singer in the Portland area, was an ideal choice to be a Santa Claus. "KA7ITR, this is K6DKA at the North Pole," said Ben.

"Yes, Santa is just coming in from outside — been feeding his reindeer."

There was the sound of a door slamming and bells and a loud whoosh of wind.

"Come on over here, Santa, and say hello to these fine boys and girls in Portland."

Kim waited with anticipation for him to change his voice into his Santa role. Just then, Ben's deep theatrical voice boomed in over the receiver.

"Ho ho ho — Merry Christmas, boys and girls! Boy, it's cold outside — looks like I'm going to have a cold trip later tonight. Mrs. Claus is just starting to pack up the gifts, so if you have any last minute requests, I'd like to know about them."

Kim pushed four-year-old Cherie in her tiny wheelchair up to the microphone. Her eyes were wide with wonder, and she stuck her thumb in her mouth when it was her time to talk. Kim knelt beside her.

"Do you want to tell Santa anything, Cherie?" Kim asked.

Cherie shook her head.

"Santa, this is Kim. I'm a friend of Cherie's and I think she wants to tell you that she wants a doll."

Cherie took her thumb out of her mouth and smiled. Kim had been quizzing the kids the last two days about special things they wanted so she could let Santa know about them ahead of time.

"One doll for Cherie Adams — brown hair — right?" Santa asked.

Cherie's mouth opened in amazement. How did Santa know?

Kim sighed in relief. She had gotten that right on the list, too.

"Well Merry Christmas, Cherie. Do you want me to bring your presents there to the hospital or to your house?"

"To my house — there's no chimney here," said Cherie, suddenly not shy. She knew that her parents had promised to be at the hospital by daybreak bringing her presents.

Another volunteer got Cherie a badge that said "I talked to Santa by Amateur Radio" and helped pin it to her robe. Kim brought the next child up to the microphone. Marc handled the transmissions smoothly, holding the mike down to the small patients beside him. A couple sat in his lap, and Kim could see the happy look on his face. She could tell that he was deeply touched by the conversations. Even the bigger kids seemed pleased to talk to Santa. When one child asked simply to 'go home,' Kim felt tears well up in her eyes.

"Well, Lisa, we'll have to see what we can do about that," Santa came back in a booming voice. "Are you taking your medicine and doing what the nurses tell you?"

Lisa giggled. Again, Kim marveled at Ben. He seemed to be able to reach across the airwaves and touch each child directly.

At 7:20, June came up to Kim and whispered in her ear.

"Why don't I take over for you here, and you go down the hall and let Joey and Shannon talk. Sam should be on frequency, now."

Kim nodded and slipped from the room. She pulled her handheld from her pocket and dialed up another simplex frequency where Santa #2, Sam Mentor, AF7S, popular local deejay, was standing by. Since the two kids who couldn't leave their rooms would not see what was going on in the lounge, they would never know that two Santas were talking at once.

Kim slipped out the door and walked down the pastel-painted hallway to Room 423. Joey Burlington, age 5, lay in the big white bed, both of his legs suspended in traction. He had fallen from his bicycle into the path of a car. He had the television on, watching an old Western rerun.

"Hi Joey," Kim said softly. "Hi — what's that?" he said, eyeing her transceiver curiously. He flicked off the television and gave her a big grin.

"It's called an Amateur Radio transceiver, Joey. We can use it to talk to people all over the world, including Santa Claus."

"Like the other kids are getting to do?" Joey asked happily.

"That's right — let's see if Santa is listening."

Kim turned the two-meter rig on, and Joey laughed at the rushing static noise it made.

"AF7S at the North Pole, this is KA7SJP — are you there Santa?"

"Is Santa one of those what-do-you-call-them — operators?" Joey asked.

Kim nodded yes as Santa came back to them.

"KA7SJP, this is Santa, AF7S. Hello Kim, how are you? Are you all ready for Christmas?"

"Yes, Santa, just about. I have a friend here who would like to talk to you. This is Joey's first time talking on Amateur Radio."

"Well hello, Joey. Merry Christmas! How old are you?"

"I'm five, Santa. I got two broken legs, Santa," Joey said clearly into the microphone. "I fell off my bike."

"Sorry to hear that, Joey, but I bet you'll be up and running around pretty soon. What do you want for Christmas?"

"A new bike," Joey said solemnly. "My bike got hurt, too."

"Well, we'll just have to see what we can do about that, Joey. But Joey, will you promise me one thing when you start riding a bike again — will you be *very* careful?"

"I *will*, Santa," Joey said.

Santa and Joey chatted a few minutes before Joey said goodbye, and Kim pinned the "I talked to Santa" badge on his pajama shirt.

Kim walked quietly across the hall to Shannon Brown's room. She felt really sorry for this six-year-old little girl who had been hospitalized all week with a severe case of pneumonia. Yesterday, she had improved enough that her parents had hoped she would be home for Christmas. But this morning, she was once again running a fever. The decision had been made to keep her in a few more days. She was still having trouble breathing and had been using oxygen.

Shannon appeared to be asleep, but Kim saw a tear rolling down her cheek. She tiptoed in and sat down quietly beside the girl. Shannon immediately opened her eyes.

"Hi Shannon — want to talk to Santa?"

Shannon rolled on her side, turning her back to Kim. Kim's heart went out to the child. The doctors had been running all sorts of tests on her, trying to figure out why she kept having recurring respiratory problems. This was her second bout with pneumonia in six months.

Kim turned on the transmitter switch.

"AF7S at the North Pole, this is KA7SJP with Shannon here at Mercy Hospital. Shannon doesn't feel much like talking right now, so I thought maybe you could just talk to her."

"Well, hello, Shannon! My goodness. How old are you? Mrs. Claus is here with me and she is busy patching the seat of my red suit. Do you know why?"

Shannon shook her head *no* and turned to lie on her back.

"Because Rudolph ate a big hole in them, that's why! I bent over to move some hay closer to him, and he bit me right on the behind!"

Shannon started to giggle and then coughed. Kim cranked the head of her bed up a little more.

"Would you like to talk to him, Shannon? Want to tell him what you want?"

"A pony," said Shannon softly.

Kim gulped. That wasn't anything on her list. Then she remembered — it wasn't a real pony, but a soft grey and white toy with a mane and tail that could be combed. That information had been carefully relayed to Shannon's parents.

"What would you name him, Shannon?" Santa asked.

"Misty," said Shannon.

"You won't name him Rudolph or Santa?" AF7S said in a pleading voice.

Shannon shook her head *no* with a big smile on her face. "You're out of luck, Santa. Looks like this pony's going to be named Misty, for sure." said Kim.

"Well, okay, Shannon. I guess that sounds like a good name. Speaking of mist, it's getting pretty foggy outside. I hope Mrs. Claus gets my pants fixed soon so I can be on my way."

"Okay, Santa, we'll let you go. Shannon, let's tell Santa Merry Christmas together."

Their voices joined together, and then Kim signed off the air.

Kim and Shannon listened to Santa's final transmission and the sound of sleigh bells jingling in the background. Kim left the room, satisfied that both children were happier after their talk with Santa.

The party was in full swing when Kim got back to the lounge. Marc was just finishing up with the last child. June was serving some kids from two big bowls on the far side of the room. When she saw Kim, she beckoned her over.

"Kim, we need some more ice for the punch. Could you run get some from the nurse's station on East Wing?" June asked.

"Sure, no problem," Kim said.

She scurried down the hall to the nurse's station. She recognized Mrs. Bradshaw, the nurse on duty, and asked her for the ice.

"Oh, I'm sorry, Kim. We're almost out. Tell you what — I know they have quite a bit up on 5th floor in the West Wing because I borrowed some earlier. Could you get that?"

"That's fine," Kim said. "I'll go get it from fifth. Kim pushed the "up" elevator button opposite the nurse's station. The elevator seemed to be delayed, and after a couple of minutes, Kim got impatient. She walked quickly to the stairwell at the end of the hall and ran up the stairs to the fifth floor.

Chapter 4

Hostage!

December 24, 7:30 p.m.
Mercy Hospital, Portland

Kim walked quickly down the fifth floor hall toward the nurse's station. The quiet on this floor was a direct contrast to the happy activity below in the fourth floor lounge. Usually there would be visitors in the halls at this hour, but tonight the place was deserted. She felt a pang of compassion for the many patients who were spending Christmas Eve alone.

Sheriff's Deputy Frank Elmo sat in a chair outside room 513, reading the newspaper. Kim had only been on this floor a few times, but she knew that 513 was where the bank robbery suspect was being held. She had visited with Officer Elmo one day in the lunchroom at the end of his shift. He had told her a little about the case. The sergeant looked up as she approached, obviously glad for any chance to break the monotony of his job.

"Merry Christmas, Officer Elmo," Kim said.

"Well hi, Kim — what are you doing here tonight?"

"Oh, we're putting on a party for the kids where they can talk to Santa by Amateur Radio," Kim explained. "I've got to hurry back," she apologized. "Just came up here to get some ice for the kid's punch."

"That sounds like a fine thing to be doing. Poor little kids being in the hospital for Christmas," said Officer Elmo.

"Well, we hope this makes it a little better," said Kim.

"I'm sure it does," he replied. "You have a good Christmas yourself."

"Thank you and you too," Kim said warmly.

She walked on down the hall and turned the corner to go down the short corridor to the West Wing nurse's station. A lone nurse, Mrs. Haskins, was on duty. Kim had met her just this morning when June took her around to various wards to visit. Mrs. Haskins looked up as Kim came to the counter.

"Hi, Kim. How's the party going?"

"Great," Kim said, pulling out her handheld two-meter rig. "Listen," she said, switching it back to the "Santa" frequency Marc was using.

Mrs. Haskins smiled as they eavesdroped on a little girl named Janine talking to Santa with Marc's help.

"That's a wonderful thing you all are doing," the nurse told Kim.

"Well it will be more wonderful if we have some ice for the punch," Kim said. "That's why I came up. Can we borrow some?"

"Sure, help yourself — it's in the freezer in there."

Kim went into the fifth-floor kitchen room and took two bags of ice from the small freezer. She came out and tried the elevator again. It seemed to be stuck on the second floor.

"I'll just take the stairs," she told Mrs. Haskins.

"Bye, Kim — you have a Merry Christmas if I don't see you again tonight to wish you one."

"You too, Mrs. Haskins."

Kim turned and walked down the corridor. It was pitch dark outside, and she could see a light rain beating against the windows as she went down the silent hall. Just as she rounded the corner leading back toward Frank, she heard the elevator doors clang open back by the nurse's station. Kim sighed. The bags of ice were sending cold shivers up her arms, but she didn't feel like going back to the elevator. She was almost to the stairs anyway.

Kim was just about to Sergeant Elmo when she heard rapid, running footsteps behind her. She turned around to look. Two men in overcoats had just come around the corner and were running at her. In one frantic moment, her eyes met theirs. The hard steely glares terrified her.

One of the men grabbed her roughly by the arm.

"You're just what we need, Nursie," he said as he propelled her down the hall in front of him.

Hearing the scuffle, Officer Elmo jumped up quickly, his hand resting on his holster.

"Pull that gun, and this girl's dead," one of the men whispered in a harsh voice.

Frank Elmo's eyes met Kim's and he slowly put his hand down. The other man reached over and quickly disarmed him.

"In there — both of you," the shorter man directed, pushing the prisoner's door open.

The minute they were inside the room, the taller man pulled a lead pipe from his belt and hit Officer Elmo over the back of the head. The sheriff's officer slumped over while Kim stood watching in horror. The other man gave a quick look out into the hall before closing the door. No one else had seen them.

The curly-haired tall man kept one hand on Kim's arm as he stood with his gun drawn by the doorway. She could feel his rough fingers pinching into her flesh.

"Please," she managed to whisper.

"Shut up!" was the terse reply.

"Willy, wake up — it's me, Joe," the shorter man was saying to the patient in the bed.

Willy groaned slightly in response and opened his eyes. Kim got her first real look at the prisoner. He was young and boyish looking with his brown hair mussed up from the pillow. Both arms were attached to intravenous tubes leading to bottles hanging on stands. In bed, he didn't look any different from any other sick person.

"Joe, is that you?" Willy said faintly.

"It sure is, Brother. We've come to get you out of here," Joe told him.

Willy raised himself up weakly on one elbow as Joe threw back the covers and tugged uselessly at iron shackles around his brother's left ankle.

Bernie, the curly-haired man, let go of Kim for a second as he stooped and rummaged through the guard's pockets. He pulled a small silver key from one and tossed it to Joe by

Willy's bed. Quickly, Joe released the leg iron and lifted Willy's pale leg free.

Kim stood absolutely still — her heart pounding so loud she thought the men would hear it. A thousand thoughts ran through her mind. She wanted to bolt for the door, but the sight of the cold steel revolver in the man's hand stopped her. Joe motioned to her to come over by the bed.

"Come over here, Nurse, and unhook him from all this stuff."

Kim looked at the maze of intravenous tubes, oxygen lines, and heart-monitor wires.

"I don't know how," she said in a whisper. "I'm not a nurse."

"She's lying," Bernie said. "Maybe she's a "nursie" — that's a little nurse," he laughed.

"Shut up, Bernie," Joe said.

Joe stared at Kim, almost as if analyzing her, and then picked up a pair of scissors off a tray and handed them to her.

"Either pull the stuff out or cut it off," he ordered.

Kim gulped and took the scissors. She laid them on the bed while she removed Willy's oxygen mask carefully. Almost instantly, his breathing quickened, and he turned anxious eyes toward Joe. His gown was half off his shoulders, and Kim could see the white bandaging around part of his chest — *a chest wound*, she thought to herself.

"You're going to kill him by doing this," she said softly.

"Let me worry about that — you just do what I say!" Joe ordered.

Kim pulled the gown down a little farther and started to pull the electrodes off Willy's chest, but Joe grabbed her wrist.

"Do that last," he said

Kim looked at him. He was smart. He must know as she did that disconnecting the heart monitor would set off some sort of alarm at the nurse's desk. She looked at the intravenous lines going into each arm.

"I've never removed an i.v.," Kim said in a shaking voice.

Impatiently, Joe picked up the scissors.

"No, don't do that," Kim begged.

But it was too late. Joe had snipped through both lines. Fluid and then blood immediately began to backflow out of the lines. Joe looked startled about the blood. The blood was staining the bed and dripping onto the floor on one side of the bed. Willy moaned and looked at his bleeding arms lying limply on the sheets.

"Joe?" he asked in a puzzled voice.

"Fix it!" Joe commanded Kim.

With trembling fingers, Kim pulled the tape off Willy's left arm and quickly pulled the needle out. Then she put the tape back in place over the needle site. She repeated the procedure on Willy's right arm. At one point, she looked up and caught Willy's clear blue eyes gazing at her.

"Who's she?" he weakly asked his brother.

"The prize that's going to get us out of here," Joe said.

Joe reached over and pulled the heart-monitor electrodes from Willy's chest. Clumsily, he tied Willy's hospital gown back in place. Kim turned her body away from them slightly and quickly reached out and slipped the scissors unseen into her pocket.

"Let's go," said Joe. He put both of Willy's arms around his neck and hoisted him up over his shoulder. Willy let out a low groan and coughed slightly.

"It's going to be okay," Joe said, reassuring him.

Willy didn't answer. His eyes were closed and his head slumped on Joe's shoulder.

At the door, Bernie grabbed Kim's arm once again and propelled her ahead of them, his gun drawn. A nurse running down the hall in response to the heart-monitor alarm froze in her tracks. She stood there with her mouth open as the men pushed Kim ahead of them into the elevator and punched the lobby button. Willy was groaning and gasping for breath. Occasionally, his eyes fluttered open. Horrified, Kim watched as his face turned a bluish color. A few drops of blood were dripping from somewhere on his body to the floor.

The elevator doors clanged open and Bernie pointed his gun out at the empty lobby. "Code White! Code White! — Main Lobby," Kim heard crackling over the public address system.

Two unarmed security men were running down the hall toward them, but they too froze when they saw the gun and the hostage situation. Watching the guards, Joe and Bernie with Kim between them, backed toward the lobby doors.

I can't go with them, Kim thought desperately as she grabbed hold of the hospital door handle and looked back down the hall toward the security police. Pain tore through her shoulder as Bernie yanked her loose and almost threw her toward the waiting van.

"A girl! What have you got a girl for?" a shrill voice rang out from the front seat.

Joe was laying Willy down in the back of the van. He tossed an old sleeping bag over him. Quickly, Bernie grabbed Kim and shoved her onto the cold metal floor of the van beside the now unconscious Willy. Then he jumped in beside the two of them while Joe ran around and climbed into the passenger side.

"Let's get out of here," he ordered the driver.

The van lurched forward, throwing Kim against the side. Instinctively, she reached in her pocket and switched the small transceiver on, turning the volume down at the same time so there would be no rush of static to alert her captors. She placed her index finger on one button of the touchtone pad on the front and then positioned her thumb on the push to talk button. Silently, she starting sending Morse code.

Frantically, she tapped out "Help, Marc, kidnapped in blue van" with her thumb. She prayed her message would reach someone. She didn't even know if Marc still had his radio on. And if he did and was still talking, the other signal would probably overshadow hers. *Help me, Marc!* she voiced silently in her mind. She wished she could just pull the radio out of her pocket and talk, but she knew that was impossible.

"What kind of driving do you call this, Sheila?" Bernie snarled at the woman driving as the van swerved back and forth across the road.

"The best I can do under the circumstances," Sheila retorted.

They were traveling at high speed through some sort of alley. Kim could catch glimpses of the backs of buildings through the high window opposite her.

"There it is. Stop back there," Joe told Sheila.

The van came to a stop.

"Why do you guys always have to steal vans? What about a Cadillac for a change?" Sheila complained. "And that one doesn't look as nice as this one. That one's gray. I like the blue better."

"Come on, Sheila," Joe said to her. "We couldn't take any chances that someone got our license plates back there. Doesn't look like anyone tailed us at all. Come on — let's get switched."

Bernie cautiously opened the back door of the van, his gun drawn. They were in a dark alley. They had pulled up next to a trash dumpster in back of a store. "Owen's Art Gallery and Framing Shop," Kim read on the painted sign over the back door.

"Get out," Bernie commanded her.

Kim edged along on the metal floor and then put her legs down over the doorway onto the ground. She shivered in the cold rain. Bernie handed Sheila his gun and told her to watch Kim while he and Joe lifted the silent Willy, wrapped in the sleeping bag, into the gray Ford van. The two women stared at each other in silence. Kim could tell Sheila was appraising her. Desperately, Kim thought of trying to tackle Sheila and run for it. But she knew that Joe also carried a gun. She didn't have a chance of making a break. Slowly, she put her hand in her pocket on the transmit button and the touchtone pad and tapped out in Morse code:

− − − O   • − − W   • E   − • N   • • • S

• − A   • − • R   − T

− − • G   • − A   • − • • L   • − • • L   • E   • − • R   − • − − Y

Then she switched the transmitter off fearing the robbers might wonder what she had in her pocket. Sheila eyed her suspiciously.

"How old are you, anyway?" Sheila asked her.

"Eighteen," Kim said softly.

"You a nurse?"

"No," Kim said. "I'm a volunteer. I was working with little kids."

"Humph," Sheila said in disgust. "If they wanted someone to help Willy and me, they should have got themselves a real nurse."

Kim noticed Sheila's bandaged left arm. So the radio reports had been true. The driver had been shot. Bernie came back around and took the gun from Sheila.

"Willy's in — wipe the van down," Joe told Bernie.

Kim watched as Bernie ran a rag over all the door handles and edges of the blue van to remove fingerprints.

Stuffing the rag in his back pocket, he walked back over to Joe.

"I'm not riding on the floor any further, that's for sure," Bernie said. "We're tying the girl up."

Kim found herself being shoved in the back of the van alongside Willy, who was breathing erratically and moaning. Bernie took off his belt. Kim winced with pain as he lashed it around her hands and tied them to a seatbelt ring in the floor. The back doors slammed shut and the two men, with Sheila in the middle, climbed in the front.

Kim tried to brace her back against the metal side of the van as they bounced along the alleyway and onto a main street. This van had no windows in the back and, with her hands tied to the floor, she couldn't peek over the front seat out the window. She settled her legs beside her and watched Willy's pale face as street lights cast an occasional beam of light onto it. Except for his shallow breathing, she would have thought he was dead.

From the traffic sounds and the smoothness of the road, Kim guessed they were on a freeway — probably Interstate-5. She had no idea if they were heading north or south. She was cold and her legs and arms were cramped from their forced positions. The reality of her helplessness sank her hopes with every mile they traveled. She closed her eyes and tried to think.

A flashlight shone in her eyes. Joe was aiming a light at Willy over the seat.

"Willy, can you hear me, Willy?" he asked.

Willy groaned just slightly.

"He's hurt a lot worse than I thought," Joe said. "There's no way we can drive all night with him like this. Go to the cabin."

"Are you crazy?" Bernie exploded.

"Yeah, Joe — I thought we were going to California tonight," Sheila said, whining.

There was silence in the van as they drove on. Then Joe's voice said quietly, "Make the turn to the cabin up here, Bernie."

Kim heard the unmistakable sound of Joe pulling back the hammer on his pistol.

Chapter 5

"Code White!"

December 24th, 8 p.m.
Mercy Hospital, Portland

T he children had all finished talking, and Marc was chatting casually with Santa, aka Ben Kingman. Some of the young patients still sat near the ham radio while others played with plastic reindeer by Santa's village. One small girl had fallen asleep in her wheelchair, her tiny hand clutched tightly around the make-believe candy cane. A Candystriper quietly wheeled her back to her room.

Jonathan sat in Marc's lap, listening to the radio conversation with keen interest. Marc had been letting him operate the volume control, and the young boy's face was lit up with happiness. Operation Santa Claus was making up for his Christmas Eve stay in the hospital.

Marc was just getting ready to sign off for the evening when suddenly a beeping tone mixed in with Ben's voice. Marc leaned forward. The beeping made it more difficult to copy Ben although Marc was used to sorting through the noise of different signals to focus on just one.

Marc sighed. Probably some guy driving down the freeway who laid his rig beside him and was accidentally keying it every time he moved. It happened to the best of hams. Wonder how long it would take for him to discover what he was doing?

"Ah, Santa, K6DKA, this is KA7ITR. Sounds like someone is holding a carrier down on you. Would you repeat that last sentence?"

But this time when Ben came back, Marc's ears focused on the beeping noise.

" • — A, • — • R, — • — • C"

This was no random noise. Someone was clearly sending Morse code. Marc looked around the lounge to see if Kim was in the room. She would love solving this mysterious transmission. No Kim — she must have run an errand for June.

"— — M,   • — A,   • — • R,   — • — • C"

Marc! Marc sat up, all of his energy directed toward the receiver.

"Stand by one, Ben — we've got a breaker," he said urgently into the microphone.

With Ben not talking, Marc was able to read the code.

"• • • • H,   • E,   • — • • L,   • — — • P"

Help! Marc stood up and grabbed a handheld two-meter rig. He quickly switched it to the simplex frequency Ben was on so he could continue listening to the code while he tried to find the sender of this distress call.

"June, where's Kim?" he yelled across the room.

June looked up at the urgency in his voice.

"She went to get ice for the punch, Marc. Ought to be back by now, though," she said, walking over to Marc. "Is something wrong?"

"Yeah, there's something wrong. Someone's calling for help in Morse code, and I think it's Kim! Where she'd go anyway?"

Just then, the emergency call "Code White" crackled over the loudspeakers. Immediately, June got up and closed the doors to the playroom.

"What's that mean?" Marc asked, looking alarmed.

"Security emergency — could just be that someone went out the emergency exit, but I need to stay with the kids until we know for sure."

"Where did Kim go?" Marc insisted.

"To the nurse's desk," June said. "Marc . . ."

Marc bolted from the room and dashed down the hall. He stopped at the four-way intersection of the two halls and then ran toward the nurse's station at the end of one corridor.

The Morse code signal was still continuing, repeating the same "Help, Marc" message. Marc held the rig to his ear as he ran. Suddenly he stopped to listen intently to the message being sent.

"— • N, • — A, • — — • P, • — — • P, • E, — • • D, — • • • B, • — • • L, • • — U, • E"

Marc strained to hear but the signal faded.

"Kim, is that you?" he shouted into the microphone.

No answer. Then the code stopped.

"Napped, blue," Marc said to himself as he continued running down the hall. "Kidnapped?"

Ginger Bradshaw, the nurse on duty, looked up as Marc raced up to the desk.

"Did Kim come here," he asked anxiously.

"Yes, she wanted some ice," Ginger said, "but we were all out so I sent her up to fifth floor. Is something wrong?" she asked. Ginger, her face an open question mark, followed Marc as he rushed into the elevator.

"Oh no," Marc groaned.

The floor inside the elevator was covered with blood droplets. Marc and Ginger sucked in their breath anxiously as the elevator made its way slowly to fifth floor. He heard the commotion before the elevator doors even opened. They ran down the hall, following a trail of blood drops around the corner and then stopped. Two policemen had cordoned off the hall. Marc watched as a doctor and a security guard lifted the unconscious Officer Elmo onto a stretcher. Two orderlies picked up the stretcher and ran with it toward the elevator.

Three Portland police officers and another sheriff's deputy were questioning a flushed looking nurse who was talking rapidly and pointing down the hall toward the elevator.

"You've got to let me through," Marc insisted frantically to the officers.

One of the police officers laid a hand on his shoulder to restrain him.

"Just a minute, son, we need to get our information first," he said.

"No!" Marc shouted. "A girl named Kim came up here, and I think she's been kidnapped!"

Hearing Marc's words, a sheriff's deputy, close to where Officer Elmo had been, motioned for the other officers to let Marc through.

"What do you know about a kidnapping?" the deputy asked Marc.

Quickly, Marc explained the code message he had heard.

"You're right — they did take her with them," a nurse said sadly.

Marc whirled and pounded his fist against the wall. The nurse came over and put her arm around him.

"Code White! Main Lobby. Code White! Main Lobby," the call crackled again over the public address system. Marc ran down the hall away from the roped-off area. He took the stairs two at a time, talking all the time to Ben on his radio.

"But she's transmitting, Ben. Maybe she can tell us where she is. Get people to cover the Portland repeaters. I'll stay on simplex."

Marc knew he would only be able to hear Kim for ten or so miles on direct simplex. Once the distance between them exceeded that, the only way to make contact would be through a repeater station.

In the lobby, things were more organized. Several law enforcement agencies had arrived on the scene. A sheriff's officer was questioning the two hospital security men who had been the last to see the escaping men and Kim. One of the officers upstairs had already radioed down that Marc was running to the lobby. A sergeant met him at the bottom of the stairs. Out of breath, Marc introduced himself. "I'm an Amateur Radio operator," Marc told him. "The girl who was kidnapped is one, too, and she just sent an emergency message in Morse code that we believe said 'kidnapped, blue.'"

"It was a blue van all right," said one of the security officers.

"Anyone get a license number?" one of the police officers asked.

"They were gone by the time we got to the door," the security officer said sadly.

The code started once again on Marc's transceiver. He held his hand up to quiet everyone. June whispered the letters aloud as the beeps came through.

"O W E N S A R T G A L L E R Y," she said. "Owens Art Gallery — where's that?"

One of the policemen was already talking into his handheld radio, reporting this new information.

"Cars are enroute now, " he said, turning to Marc. "Would you come with me so you can continue to monitor her messages?"

Marc quickly agreed and ran with two of the officers to a waiting police car in front of the hospital. He climbed in the back seat, still clutching his two-meter rig to his ear. He tried transmitting to Kim, but there were no more signals as the police car careened its way through the back streets toward the art gallery.

Marc saw the blue van as soon as they turned into the alleyway.

"Stay here, and that's an order," the police officer told Marc as he got out and crouched beside the car.

Marc watched as the officers carefully converged on the van and searched the recesses of the alleyway. In a few minutes, one of them came back to Marc and told him he could get out.

"Any more signals?" he asked Marc.

"No," Marc told him. "Nothing at all."

He walked over to the back of the empty van. The flashing blue lights from the police car bathed the alleyway in ghostly luminance. Marc looked in at the blood-stained floor that officers were examining with flashlights.

"Find out anything, Mike?" one of the officers asked another who was walking back from his patrol car.

"It's stolen all right — taken two days ago from a neighborhood not too far from here. We're running a list right now of all the vehicles stolen in this area this week — especially those reported missing today. That may give us a clue as to what the suspects are driving now."

"Probably another van, don't you think, Mike? Considering there are five of them and one of them badly injured," one officer said.

"Likely," was all Mike replied.

They stood around waiting for the crime detection unit to arrive to take fingerprints from the van and tow it to the police garage.

Marc shifted anxiously from foot to foot, the receiver still at his ear. Not a sound. He switched to a Portland repeater frequency where he thought Ben might be.

"K6DKA, this is KA7ITR — are you on frequency, Ben?"

"KA7ITR from K6DKA — sure am, Marc. Any news?"

"None," said Marc. "How about you?"

"Not a peep," Ben told him. "But we'll keep listening in shifts around the clock.

"Come on, Marc. There's nothing more to be done here. We'll take you back to the hospital," one of the officers said.

They drove in silence back to Mercy Hospital. Officer Mike Hurd went back in the building with Marc.

"So what are you going to do now?" Marc asked.

"First, we need to talk to everyone who had any contact with the robbers tonight. Then a description of them will be sent out to all law enforcement agencies in the state," Officer Hurd told him.

A hospital security officer interrupted them.

"We're meeting in June Blakely's office — follow me."

Feeling emotionally and physically drained, Marc clenched his teeth and walked down the long hall to June's office.

Chapter 6

Night Drive

December 24th 8 - 11 p.m.
On the road somewhere

"I ain't driving anywhere until you put that gun away," Bernie told Joe as he pulled the van over to the side of the road.

Joe kept the gun pointed, trigger cocked, at Bernie.

"Let's get a few things straight, Bernie," Joe told him quietly. "I'm running this show. I'm the one who's got the connections in California, and I'm the one who can get us across the border. But I'm not going anywhere until Willy can travel. Now if you want to get out here and be on your own, you're welcome to do just that."

"Yeah, sure, without any of the money, right?" Bernie grumbled.

"There's hardly any money left," Sheila wailed. "You're not going to let him take our money, are you, Joe?"

"Don't you ever shut up?" Bernie said angrily to Sheila.

"Just make your choice, Bernie," Joe said quietly.

Reaching down to savagely scratch his leg, Bernie growled something unintelligible. He lit a cigarette, started the van, and pulled back onto the freeway. Kim couldn't see the road signs, but she felt the van leave the main road and head to the right. She braced herself as they went down a long curved offramp. They made several stops at stop signs — *must be going through a town of some sort,* she thought. Then it got black again and the van picked up speed. Willy groaned every time they went around a curve in the road. Kim could see him struggling to breathe.

She wrestled with her conscience. *What do I care if he dies?* she asked herself. But she found that she did care and not just because some gut level fear told her that her own survival was tied to his. It just wasn't in her nature not to help someone if she could. Timidly, she spoke up.

"Your brother could breathe better if you would prop him up on something," she said quietly.

The three passengers in the front seat jumped at her voice. Joe turned around and shone a flashlight in her face. Kim squinted under the bright light.

"He's having trouble breathing — look at him," Kim said. "If you put something under his shoulders, it would be easier for him."

Joe turned the light on his brother who groaned softly. Joe struggled in the front seat taking off his coat.

"Sheila, take off your coat, too" he ordered.

"I'm cold. I don't think that heater works," she muttered.

"Just take it off," Joe demanded, reaching over to help her slip her injured arm out of the sleeve.

He rolled the two coats up and leaned awkwardly over the back seat. Kim wondered if Bernie might seize this opportunity to grab Joe's gun, but he continued driving. From what she could see of the back of his head, she guessed that his eyes were straight forward on the road. Joe shoved the coats under Willy's shoulders covered by the sleeping bag. Willy moaned at the movement.

"Okay?" Joe said to Kim.

"He needs to be in a hospital," Kim said quietly.

Joe turned around and ignored her. The van continued on through the night. There was another town they went through — more stop signs than the first. Occasionally, the neon lights of a fast food restaurant cast a reddish glow into the dark van. *Why aren't we stopped by the police?* Kim thought. Had anyone gotten the license of the van in their getaway? She strained to loosen her hands from the belt tying them to the floor. If only she could transmit so that someone might have a chance of tracking her signal. Her wrists ached from their awkward position. Once again, Kim spoke up.

"My hands really hurt. Is there any chance you could untie them?" she said to Joe's back.

Joe turned to look at her.

"Shut up!" was all he said.

Kim shivered at the tone of his voice. She lowered her head to her knees and closed her eyes. She had no idea how long they drove on, but it seemed like hours. Her feet went to sleep, and she struggled to put her legs in a new position that wasn't so cramped. They crossed some railroad tracks with a jolt that made Willy wake up briefly and groan.

Then they turned off whatever road they were on to a smaller winding one. Bernie took a lot of the curves too fast, and Willy moaned and coughed.

"I'm gonna be sick if you don't slow down," Sheila complained.

"First you're hungry; then you're carsick — what's with you, anyway?" Bernie growled.

"Just take it a little easy on the corners, Bernie," Joe told him.

Bernie snickered and lit a cigarette. Kim closed her eyes and listened to the occasional conversation among the occupants of the front seat. They were an odd group for sure. Bernie was the one who scared her the most. He didn't seem to have any humanity about him at all. Joe wasn't much better, but he obviously had feeling for his brother, and she guessed also for Sheila. It seemed like Sheila annoyed them both though. What a bimbo she seemed to be, and yet Kim sensed an evilness beneath the dumb exterior. Willy was an unknown —just an injured man.

The van slowed slightly, and Kim was able to brace her back against the side so that she could keep her balance better. She wondered where they were. Her ears weren't popping at all, and she hadn't felt the sensation of climbing, so she doubted they were in the mountains. Since the mountains were to the east, that left north, south, or west. The interstate highway ran north and south. She knew they weren't still on that, but they could be on parallel side roads. However, her best guess, due to the curves in the road, was that they were heading west toward the coast somewhere.

The van bounced off the pavement onto a dirt road of some kind. They went up an incline and then down the other side. Bernie brought the van to a jarring stop.

"Home sweet home," muttered Sheila. "Wonder if the electricity is still on?"

"Yeah, my cousin, Bob, leaves it on all year so the pump stays running," said Joe.

"Does he know we're here?" Sheila whined.

"Naw," Joe reassured her. "He goes to Florida every winter — won't be back until Easter."

"Are we just going to sit here and talk or are we going in?" Bernie asked, lighting another cigarette.

Kim heard the front doors slam shut. Joe opened the double back doors of the van and shone the flashlight on Willy. Willy opened his eyes.

"Joe?" he asked. "Where . . .?"

"At the cabin, Willy, where we all used to go fishing. Remember the cabin?"

But Willy had lapsed back into unconsciousness. Gingerly, Bernie and Joe tucked the sleeping bag around Willy and then lifted his limp body from the van to carry it into the cabin. Kim sat, still tied to the metal floor, shivering in the damp winter cold. There was something dark on the floor where Willy had been lying. She guessed it might be blood. She shuddered. There was no way a badly injured person could survive this kind of treatment.

Kim peered out the open back of the van, but there was total darkness. The forlorn hooting call of an owl wafted through the night.

Joe came back to the van. He reached in and quickly untied Kim's hands.

"Come on," he said, roughly grabbing her arm and pulling her across the metal floor.

Kim's legs were so stiff from sitting that she stumbled for a few steps, but Joe held her up and pushed her along the uneven gravel path toward the cabin. There was a dim light coming from behind one of the shuttered windows. The wind rustling through the tall trees and the smell of salt air left no doubt in Kim's mind that they were fairly near the coast.

Joe pulled the battered wooden door open and shoved her into the cabin. One small lamp dimly lit the main room of the structure. Willy had been put on a sagging couch next to the wall. Sheila sat on a wooden chair near a pot-bellied woodstove that Bernie was loading with kindling. There wasn't much time for Kim to look at anything, as Joe took her arm and pushed her toward a door by the woodstove.

"You'll be staying downstairs," he said.

"In the executive suite," Sheila laughed.

Joe shoved her through the doorway, and Kim put her right hand out against the cold cement wall to steady herself as they went down the creaking wooden steps into the damp musty cellar. Joe shone the flashlight ahead of them so that she could see her steps. At the bottom of the stairs was another door.

"There's no light in there, but there's a bed against the wall. Toilet and sink on the other — we used to sleep down here as kids," Joe told her.

He put his hand on her back and pushed her into the room. Then he pulled the door shut behind her. Kim heard him fastening a latch of some kind on the other side.

Kim stood motionless inside the room as the dank, musty air assailed her nose. She was shivering so hard from both the cold and her fear that her teeth chattered. She felt hot tears spring into her eyes, but she wiped them away with the back of her hand.

If I'm going to live, I have to use my head, she told herself fiercely. She blinked her eyes, trying to see anything in the darkness. A tiny shaft of moonlight peeked in through some sort of an opening on the opposite wall. The light did nothing to illuminate the room, but Kim hoped that if she could get right over next to it, she might be able to see something. She put her hand out and started feeling her way along the damp wall to the right of her.

"Ouch!" she exclaimed as her shins raked against the metal edges of a bed frame.

She put her hands down and felt the lumpy bed in the corner of the room. It was covered by a sleeping bag that felt damp to the touch. The strong odor of mildew sickened Kim, but she swallowed hard and kept on moving along the bed. The end of the bed touched the adjoining wall, and Kim followed the wall with her hands. Midway along that wall, she ran into a curtain which she pulled aside and groped behind. It seemed to be blank space. She stepped into it and clothes on hangers brushed her face. Kim felt them with her hands — several flannel shirts and some khaki-feeling pants. She grabbed one of the shirts and put it around her trembling shoulders.

She explored the other side of the closet and ran into a sink. The toilet was right next to it. As Kim bent over to feel the fixtures clear to the floor, the scissors and transceiver in her pocket poked into her leg. *If they find these on me, I'm a goner,* she thought. Quickly, she pulled them out. She lifted the toilet tank lid and dropped the scissors into the cold water and then quietly replaced the lid. The transceiver was another problem. Kim backtracked out of the bathroom/closet and felt her way back to the bed. She tucked the transceiver in the foot of the sleeping bag.

Once again, she felt her way along the wall — this time past the bathroom area to the slit where she had seen the moonlight. It was completely dark now. Kim patted the wall with her hands all the way to the low ceiling. Cobwebs wrapped around her fingers. She wanted to pull her hands back in disgust, but she kept exploring.

The window, such as it was, was a strip of glass about four inches wide at the top of a boarded-up area. Kim stood on her tiptoes to try and see out. Total blackness. The moon must have been peeking through some clouds, before, and now it was gone. She continued her exploration along the last wall.

Her knees ran into a metal box anchored to the floor. Kim crouched and felt its outline with her hands. A stove of some kind — probably a wood stove. She patted the top until her fingers found a six inch round pipe leading from the stove to the ceiling. By putting her ear next to the pipe, she could hear the rumble of their voices upstairs. No words were distinguishable, but she could hear Sheila's whining voice, and Bernie's angry retort.

Kim backed away from the stove and groped for the wall beside it. Almost instantly, she was back at the door. She tugged on it, but it was fastened tight. A few more feet and she stumbled on the bed frame again.

Kim began a circle of the room again, this time with her hands over her head feeling the low ceiling. She hated all the spider webs, but she knew what she was looking for. Right in the middle, she found it: an empty light socket. So there was the possibility of light down here, after all. She wondered if there would be any chance of talking Joe into giving her a light-bulb — that was assuming this crummy place had more than the one she had seen upstairs.

Slowly she made her way back to the bed again. Trying not to inhale the rank odor of the sleeping bag, Kim slipped inside it and pulled it up around her. Her foot touched her ham transceiver, and she reached down and grabbed it.

Hopefully, she looked back toward where she remembered the window. Still no light. The shaft of moonlight must have gotten through a momentary break in the clouds. Now she could hear rain pelting against the sides of the cabin and on the stove pipe which obviously ran through to the roof. She doubted there would be any more chances for light until the storm passed.

Kim switched her rig on and held it close to her ear. She had last had it on a Portland repeater frequency. She pushed the button which would move the frequency higher and then pushed the transmit button to see if she could break into a repeater. Nothing. *If only I knew the repeater frequencies by heart,* she thought. But she didn't, so she would have to continue in this hit or miss fashion.

To get her signal out, Kim knew she would have the best chance over by the window, so reluctantly she left the dubious warmth of the sleeping bag and made her way back around the room.

Frantically, she punched up frequency after frequency with no results. To try all the possible combinations would take a long time — she prayed she would get lucky.

The sound of heavy footsteps coming down the stairs startled her so much she almost dropped the transceiver. Panic stricken, Kim groped her way back to the bed and was just able to shove the two-meter rig back in the sleeping bag as the door opened. She was still standing beside the bed.

It was Bernie. He directed the flashlight first at the bed and then swept the room with it. Its beam caught her and she blinked in the brightness aimed at her face.

"Well, well, well, aren't you the gorgeous one with that shirt on?" he said.

He reached out to grab her arm and Kim quickly shrugged his hand off.

"Don't like me, huh, Nursie? Well, Joe said to bring you on upstairs, so you'd better hustle. When Joe says to do something, we do it!" Bernie said sarcastically.

He stood in the doorway, motioning for her to go through ahead of him. Warily keeping her eye on Bernie, Kim side-stepped through the door and started up the steps.

Chapter 7

"Nursie"

December 25th — 1:00 a.m.
In the cabin

Kim scurried up the stairs, keeping her distance ahead of Bernie. She pushed on the door at the top, but the warped wood refused to budge. Bernie laughed and calmly reached across her, leaning his shoulder against the door. The door popped open and the two of them entered the small living area.

Joe looked up from the stool where he was sitting in the shadows by Willy. He didn't say a word to Kim who stood shivering by the wall. Her lips were trembling, and she wrapped her arms tightly around herself. After a few awkward minutes of silence, Joe motioned for her to stand by the woodstove. She walked over to the blazing fire and turned her back to the welcome heat while she surveyed the scene in the small rundown cabin.

Willy, who appeared to be asleep on a sagging couch in the corner, was still wrapped in the same sleeping bag Joe had covered him with in the van. His face wasn't visible in the dim light, but the sound of his labored breathing filled the room. Sheila was asleep in the rocking chair by the woodstove, a ragged blanket over her. Kim couldn't see Joe's face but could feel his stare. It gave her a creepy feeling. Bernie had disappeared into a small bathroom off the living room. Now, he came back into the room and crawled back into a sleeping bag on the floor. Kim watched Joe, waiting to see what he wanted of her.

"Bernie and I are hungry," Joe said. "Fix us some grub."

He motioned to a small kitchen at the far end of the room. Kim stood silently by the fire, just staring at Joe.

"Well, go on, fix us some grub," he commanded, waving his gun at her.

Reluctantly, she left the heat of the stove and walked into the small windowless alcove of a kitchen where she shuddered in revulsion at the dirtiness everywhere. The one small counter had a coating of dried food remnants, and the two-burner stove was thick with grease. A big hole in the grimy vinyl floor marked the spot where a refrigerator had once been.

Gingerly, Kim opened the wall cupboard beside the stove. An assortment of dented and cracked tin pans was strewn on the sticky wooden shelves. She reached up and opened the other cupboard on the other wall. A crumpled plastic bag labeled Calcora Rice lay in shreds at the front of the shelf. Kim pulled it out and gasped.

It was full of mouse droppings. So mice had finished off what was left of the rice. *They probably left a long time ago though. Smart mice,* Kim thought.

She stood on her tiptoes and squeamishly reached her hand to the back of the shelves. There were some cans back there. She grabbed one and pulled it out. Canned chili. She reached in and got another. More canned chili. She pulled each one out — seven total — and lined them up on the counter. Three of chili, two of chicken noodle soup, two of peaches, and one of green beans.

Kim picked up one can of chili and one of soup. She turned and showed them to Joe.

"Soup," he said.

Kim opened a drawer by the sink. A rusty can opener and a few pieces of battered silverware lay tumbled in the drawer. She pulled out the can opener and turned on the water in the sink to wash it off. No hot water. She let it run some more. Still cold. Joe heard the water running and yelled at her.

"If you're trying to get hot water, don't bother. The water heater busted five years ago."

Kim looked under the sink. A small container of powdered soap poked out from the cobwebs in the back of the cupboard. She retrieved it and poured some on the can opener and then scrubbed it the best she could with her hands under the icy, cold well water. She also washed off the top of the soup can before opening it.

The small tin pan she pulled from the cupboard actually didn't look too dirty, but Kim washed it anyway. To her surprise, both of the burners on the stove worked and in a few minutes, the familiar smell of chicken noodle soup permeated the air. Kim looked in the cupboard for some bowls. There weren't any, but she found four cracked cups. She poured soup into two of them and took them to the men.

Joe said gruffly, "If there's any left, eat it yourself."

"I think you've gone soft in the head," Bernie growled.

Kim slipped back into the kitchen. In spite of all her fear, she found she was hungry. She poured the last half cup of soup into another cup and drank it quickly. Then she washed the cup and pan in the cold water. Uncertain of what she was to do now, she stood in the doorway watching the men. Willy was groaning and thrashing on the couch. He opened his eyes and looked at Joe.

"Joe? Is that you? Where are we?"

"In the cabin, Willy," Joe told him. "We're just resting for a day or so, and then we're heading for Mexico. How about some soup, Willy?"

"No," Willy said, shaking his head. "My chest hurts *so bad.*"

Joe got up and pulled the sleeping bag off his brother. The front of the hospital gown was soaked with blood. It was starting to seep into the couch cushion below him.

"Where'd all this come from?" Joe said angrily. "I didn't know you were bleeding like this."

Willy raised up slightly to look at the front of his gown and moaned. Kim strained to see more of what was going on but could see only their forms from the doorway. Joe kicked Bernie.

"Wake up Bernie — look at all this blood. Did you know Willy was bleeding like this?"

"Yeah, he's been dripping ever since you carted him out of the hospital. What about it?" Bernie said and rolled back over on his side.

Kim could see the fury on Joe's face. His hand fingered the gun stuck into the waistband of his pants. Bernie started snoring. Joe looked up and caught Kim's gaze.

"Come here, Nursie," he said quietly.

"I told you before — I'm not a nurse; I'm a volunteer," Kim said, walking over to the couch.

"You got a uniform on — you must know something. Fix my brother up," Joe ordered.

Kim crouched beside the bed and looked at Willy. His face was ashen, even in the pale light. There was a lot of blood, but she didn't think he was hemorrhaging. He must be leaking slowly from a wound somewhere. Obviously, Joe hadn't seen the blood in the darkness of the van with Willy covered by the sleeping bag. Kim hadn't, either, but Bernie had. She wondered why Bernie hadn't said anything. A cold chill swept through her as she thought of how evil he was.

"Was your brother shot?" Kim asked.

"Yeah, he was shot all right," Joe said. "Fell down right behind me in the bank."

Kim reached forward and put her fingers on Willy's limp wrist. His pulse was weak and rapid. His eyes fluttered open at her touch.

"Who are *you*?" he said weakly.

"My name is Kim. Did you have an operation on your chest, Willy?"

"Yeah, I guess so. I can't think so good now," he whispered and then closed his eyes.

Kim bent over and untied the gown from behind his neck. Her knowledge of medical treatment consisted of basic first aid classes she had taken with the ARES (Amateur Radio Emergency Services) group. She had never even seen a gunshot wound.

Carefully, she pulled the gown to the bottom of his ribs. He'd had surgery all right. A suture line extended right up the middle of his chest, and right in the middle of it was a two-inch opening where the metal sutures had pulled loose. Blood and fluid were slowly seeping out the open wound. She noticed a small stitched cut on his left side and wondered if some kind of chest tube had been in there. A drainage tube was stitched into the bottom of the incision and blood dripped from that, too. Kim knew enough about hospital procedures to know that the drainage was normal. But the bleeding from the incision had to be stopped.

"Have you got any sheets or towels? Anything *clean* in this place?" she asked.

Joe got up and went into the bathroom Bernie had been in earlier. He came back carrying a grayish, mildewed towel. Kim looked at it and sighed.

"I need a knife," she told Joe.

"What for?" he asked her suspiciously.

"To make some bandages."

Joe pulled a knife out of his back pocket and handed it to her. Kim opened it and cut the edge of the towel to tie into strips. The towel was so filthy — she just couldn't put that next to an open wound. She took the knife and cut into her own Candystriper skirt, ripping out a one-foot square.

It wasn't sterile but it would have to do. She folded the red and white material into a square. Then she took one of the towel strips and folded it into a square of about the same size. She put the clean skirt material on top of Willy's wound and then put the bulkier wad of toweling on top.

"You'll have to help me," she said to Joe. "We need to put pressure on that hole. Lift him up so I can put these towel strips under him and tie them around his chest to hold the pad in place."

Joe stood up and put both of his hands gently under Willy's sides. He raised him carefully, but, even so, Willy let out a huge groan as Kim quickly tied the makeshift pressure bandage in place. Joe laid Willy back on the bed, and Kim watched the pad on his chest for signs of bleeding. The blood stained through but then slowed dramatically.

"I think that will eventually stop it," Kim said as she pulled Willy's gown back up around his neck.

Willy opened his eyes and fastened his gaze on Kim. She was startled by the intensity of his blue eyes. *Why, he looks like a boy my age,* she thought. She looked at Joe. There was a resemblance, but it was very faint. Joe looked so hardened, while Willy could have been one of her college friends. She wondered how old he was — early twenties, she guessed.

"Thank you," Willy murmured weakly and then closed his eyes.

"Willy, could you drink some water?" Kim asked.

"Yeah, I'm really thirsty," he said, opening his eyes again.

Kim went to the kitchen and filled one of the cups with water. Putting one hand behind Willy's head, she lifted it so that he could drink. He was too weak to hold the cup, so she held it for him. He took a couple of sips and then lay back on the bed.

Turning to Joe, Kim told him, "One of those lines you cut from his arm was giving him fluid. If he's going to stay alive, he'll need some water every couple of hours."

Joe stared at her.

This is crazy, Kim told herself. *Here I am giving instructions like I'm training nurses, and this guy would just as soon kill me as not.*

Willy was moaning and coughing. Each cough obviously hurt. As Kim looked at him, she wondered how bad his injury was; had the bullet touched his heart? Penetrated a lung? How was she to know what damage lay under those stitches?

"I think you should prop him up all the time," Kim said to Joe. "Makes it easier for him to breathe."

Joe's eyes searched the room and finally stopped on the blanket covering Sheila. He got up and pulled it from her which brought a howl of complaint. Ignoring her, Joe brought the blanket to Kim.

"Here," she said taking the dirty camp blanket from Joe and rolling it up. "Lift the cushion, and I'll slip this under him."

Willy cried out again as Joe lifted the cushion and Kim stuffed the blanket in under his shoulders. But when he settled back down, he opened his eyes again and nodded his head slightly. Kim pulled the sleeping bag up over his shoulders.

"Oow my arm! It's gonna fall off!" came a cry from the corner. "And now, I'm freezing, too."

Joe's sigh was obvious before he got up to tend to Sheila. He walked over to her and bent to examine her arm by the light of the stove. Kim eyed the front door anxiously. She wondered if she could make a break for it. Probably, Joe would shoot her before she ever reached the door. No, she would have to wait until the time was right. She prayed there would be a "right" time.

"You better look at her, too, Nursie," Joe said.

"She ain't touching me!" Sheila said in a high voice.

Kim stood a couple of feet behind Joe. She didn't intend to touch Sheila unless she absolutely had to. Joe insisted. Sheila refused. The battle went on between the two of them for several minutes. Finally, Joe took Sheila's injured arm in his right hand and motioned with his left to Kim. Kim came over near the stove, trying to avoid Sheila's hostile gaze.

Joe unwrapped the pillowcase bandage above Sheila's elbow. There was a bloody purple furrow across the fleshy part of her arm. It didn't look very deep to Kim, and she guessed that a bullet had just grazed her. What was of concern was the angry-looking red puffy tissue all around the wound.

"It's infected," Kim said quietly. "Do you have any disinfectant, like peroxide?"

Joe motioned toward the bathroom with his head.

"Go look in there," he said.

Kim opened the door of the small bathroom.

"Pull the string in the middle for light," Joe called after her.

Kim groped around for the string and finally found it. The dim dirty lightbulb did little to illuminate the room, but at least Kim could see the cabinet above the sink. She opened it and several used razor blades fell out into the washbowl. The cupboard was in the same state of disarray and grime as those of the kitchen. She pawed through empty aspirin bottles to see what was in the back. A brown plastic bottle with no label lay on its side.

When Kim opened it and smelled it, there was a faint odor of iodine. She poured a little on her finger — dark brown.

"Is this iodine?" she asked Joe, taking the bottle back to him.

"Yeah, Uncle Bill used to doctor his hunting dog with that stuff when he'd get cut in barbed wire."

"How old is it?" Kim asked.

"I don't know — fifteen years, maybe twenty," Joe said.

"Here," Kim said, handing it to him. "Pour some of it on her arm. It might help."

Sheila yelled as Joe poured the brown iodine on the wound, although Kim doubted it still had any potency left to it. Then he wrapped the pillowcase strips back around it. Sheila glared at Kim. Kim stared back.

"You need medical care just like Willy does," Kim said.

"You might lose your arm if you don't get it."

"You hear that, Joe? Lose my arm!" Sheila shrieked.

"Aw, she's just trying to scare you, aren't you, Nursie?" Joe said.

Kim was silent. Bernie reached out and grabbed the iodine bottle from Joe.

"Give me some of that stuff," he growled, raising his pant leg and slopping the brown liquid on the raised red blisters on his skin.

"Well, Bernie — I do believe you've got yourself a regular ole case of Poison Oak," Sheila said, her tears turning to laughter.

"Shut up," Bernie said, but he took some more of the liquid and rubbed it on the inside of one arm and then pulled up his shirt and put some on his stomach. Even Joe laughed.

"What have you been doing? Rolling in the stuff?" Joe asked.

"It's your fault!" Bernie told Joe angrily. "You were the one that had us hide for hours out in those blackberries. I guess I got into this stuff when I was walking around out there."

Joe didn't say anything, but after a few minutes, he picked up the flashlight and pointed toward the door leading to the basement. Silently, Joe and Kim made their way down the stairs. He opened the door at the bottom and reached out to grab Kim's arm.

"I can go in on my own," she said.

She heard the door latch behind her. The cold dankness enveloped her, and this time there was no stopping the tears. She sat down on the bed and buried her face in her hands.

"What a way to spend *Christmas*," she sobbed quietly.

The thought of her family in their warm home sent pangs of longing through her. In her mind, she could see every detail of their living room, but overshadowing that scene was the image of her family and Marc frantic with worry.

I bet they're all half-crazy with worry, Kim thought. *And I bet Marc and every ham in the state are listening to every frequency known to man.*

"I won't disappoint them," Kim said aloud. "I'm going to get out of this."

She got up and felt her way to the closet. Quickly, she discarded her skirt and slipped on the khaki pants. Then she put a jacket over the flannel shirt. Her shivering eased under the extra layers. She made her way back to the bed and retrieved her radio from the sleeping bag.

She punched up the next frequency. Nothing. Next one. Nothing. Kim set her jaw with determination. She would not give up!

Chapter 8

A Sad Christmas Eve in Salem

Christmas Eve — 10:30 p.m.
Kim Stafford's house in Salem

Marc put on his turn indicator to exit from I-5 onto the Salem offramp. He'd had a long, miserable drive from Portland, reviewing the events of the past two hours and wondering if the police had told the Staffords what had happened to their daughter.

After standing around with June and other hospital employees being interviewed by law enforcement officers, Marc had finally announced that he wanted to go to Kim's parents and tell them, personally. Representatives from each agency took his name and number and set up times that Marc would call them to check-in. He called his own parents to relate the sad news. They both offered to come down and help, but Marc told them he would call if there was anything they could do. He walked back to the lobby and gave June an emotional hug goodbye. She walked out to the parking lot with him.

"We have to hold positive thoughts, Marc," she told him.

Marc tried to answer, but his throat felt so tight he couldn't talk. June rubbed his shoulder sympathetically and waved goodbye as he climbed into his car to make the hour-long drive south. Now he was almost to the Staffords.

"Kim, oh Kim," he whispered as he drove through the rain and darkness. The twinkling Christmas lights on stores and houses seemed like an insult to the despair he felt. Just three short hours ago the two of them had been so happy, working with the kids and looking forward to spending more of the evening together. In an instant, joy had turned to tragedy. What would he say to her family?

He listened hopefully to the various repeater frequencies, but, except for an occasional check-in of hams who were already monitoring the emergency, all was quiet. Marc took a deep breath as he drove down the familiar street to Kim's house. A strange white car was in the driveway so he parked at the curb. Rain pelted him as he ran across the sidewalk to Kim's driveway. Then he saw the insignia on the side of the white car: Marion County Sheriff's Department.

So they had beaten him here. Marc felt relief that he wouldn't be the first to break the news to Kim's parents. He knocked on the door and was surprised when Lt. Baxter opened it. Lt. Baxter was the Sheriff's officer who had helped in the search that had rescued Marc last May from Mt. Jefferson when he had broken his leg hiking.

"Hello, Marc," Lt. Baxter said taking Marc's hand in both of his. "I saw the teletype when it came into Dispatch Center, and since I know the family, I came over to see what I could do to help. Mr. and Mrs. Stafford are in the living room."

Marc walked to the living room. Kim's father was pacing back and forth impatiently while her mother sat on the couch crying silently. She saw Marc and stood up. Without a word, they hugged each other. Marc felt his own eyes burn with tears as he tried to think of something to say. Between the emotion he felt now and the heart-pounding adrenaline experience he'd been through in the last two hours, Marc found himself shaking. He drew a deep breath and tried to steady his voice as he spoke slowly.

"The Amateur Radio operators have activated emergency nets," he told the Staffords. "They're monitoring every frequency Kim might use."

They all sat down, and Marc told the events of the evening leading up to the kidnapping. He related all the details of Kim's emergency transmissions and his drive with the police to the alley where the robbers had switched vans. Mr. Stafford sat quietly, clenching and unclenching his hands. Brandon, Kim's younger brother, appeared in the doorway.

"Hi, Marc," he said as he came to sit next to him. His usual teasing personality was absent as he sat staring at the unlit Christmas tree surrounded with gaily wrapped gifts.

"Can the hams track Kim's signal?" he asked Marc.

"Maybe, if she transmits long enough," Marc told him. "But we haven't heard anything from her since they changed vans in the alleyway."

"What if the bank robbers have Kim's radio and are listening?" asked Mr. Stafford.

"That's a possibility I thought about on the way down here," Marc said. "That's why I'd like to set up packet radio so that we could run net control by computer without the possibility of anyone other than Amateur Radio operators intercepting the messages.

Brandon's eyes brightened.

"That's what Mom and Dad are giving Kim for Christmas: a packet setup — it's right there under the tree!" he said pointing to a box wrapped in green paper with red ribbon.

Suddenly an idea occurred to Marc.

"Mr. and Mrs. Stafford — I was going to go home to my own packet equipment, but I know Kim has a computer similar to mine. It wouldn't take long to get her equipment on the air. If you want, I could establish net control right here, and that way you could watch everything that's going on."

"Yes! do it, please," Mr. Stafford said as he handed the package to Marc.

Marc hesitated a minute and then took the paper off. It was a AEA Packratt PK 232 just like he had at home.

"Her Uncle Steve recommended this one," said Mrs. Stafford. "I'm afraid we don't know much about it, not even how it works."

As Marc took the equipment out of the box, he explained the basics of packet radio to them quickly. He told them how packet was a way of linking computers with Amateur Radio so that hams could sit and talk to each other on their computer screens. If one of the operators wasn't there, the computer could still take messages and pass them on to other destinations. He added that hams have set up packet bulletin boards all over the world, and that messages are automatically forwarded over the radio from one computer to the next until they reach their final destination. It was the perfect medium for handling an emergency such as Kim's where multiple messages might be coming in from all over the state.

Lt. Baxter listened with interest, too. Packet radio had been used as part of the emergency communications in a recent flood at the coast. The effective handling of emergency traffic by Amateur Radio operators had further cemented the bond between them and law enforcement agencies.

"I'm going to put your name, Marc, and the Staffords phone number here down as a contact," Lt. Baxter said. "We'll be calling you frequently for updates and expect you to call us the minute you hear anything."

Marc nodded in agreement. Lt. Baxter stood and shook hands with all of them.

"The FBI is involved too, now, because of the bank robbery. Every law enforcement agency in the state is on alert. I wish I could reassure you more, but I promise you we'll do everything we can to get your daughter back unharmed."

Mrs. Stafford was crying again. Lt. Baxter patted her shoulder and then left to return to headquarters.

Marc carried the equipment upstairs to Kim's room and set to work immediately. Brandon brought him a screwdriver and adjusted a desk lamp so Marc could see to hook up the PK 232 to Kim's "base station." Fortunately, the feed line for her base station was located within easy reach of the computer so they didn't have to run any extra cable. Within an hour, Marc had everything put together.

"If Kim's Uncle Steve made the list for your parents of what to give her, he made a good one," he said to Brandon approvingly. "They've given her a TNC, the software, and the cables to hook it all together — everything she needs."

Brandon smiled as Marc continued talking to himself. He'd heard Kim joke about Marc's habit of thinking aloud.

"Let's see," said Marc. "I could connect to the emergency bulletin board run by ARES (Amateur Radio Emergency Services) at the state capitol. The program on that allows conference calls where everyone receives messages at the same time. But — hmmm —," he said scratching his head. "I think I'm going to have so many people involved that I'll want to be selective in what information I send to each person. I wish I had 'Lan-Link' (computer program written especially for use with packet radio) — that would be the perfect program."

"Just a minute, Marc," Brandon said.

He ran downstairs and came back in a few minutes with another wrapped gift. It was addressed to Kim from Uncle Steve.

"This is Lan-Link," Brandon said.

"Gee, how do you know what everyone is getting?" Marc said, shaking his head in amazement.

"I have Xray vision," Brandon said, grinning for the first time that night.

Marc installed the software and connected with the Salem packet bulletin board. He left a bulletin to the local hams about the nature of the emergency. Then he sent similar messages to the ARES net control in each county and asked that hams listen for Kim on both simplex and the nearest repeater. Marc remembered how he had frantically switched back and forth from simplex (direct) to duplex (through a repeater station) when he'd been injured. Kim might be trying the same thing.

If anyone heard anything, he was to contact the net control person who could forward that information by packet to Marc via the Salem node (A node is like a repeater for packet). He also established times for voice check-ins on the repeaters he could hear on two meters. That would keep voice transmissions to a minimum — especially those that contained any clues about the location of the robbers.

One of the beauties of the packet system was that operators who were outside of his repeater range could send messages to him. The messages were forwarded automatically from node to node. Marc looked at the international time clock above Kim's rig and jotted down the check-in times on a pad of paper.

Mrs. Stafford appeared in the doorway with a cup of hot chocolate.

"I called your mom and dad to tell them you were spending the night with us," she said. "They asked for you to call them if we hear anything, no matter what time it is."

"Sure," said Marc reaching out to take the cup of chocolate from Mrs. Stafford.

"You know," she said, wiping away tears, "the last time I brought hot chocolate to Kim's room was last spring when she sat up all night listening for you."

"And she saved my life," Marc said quietly. "Now it's my turn."

Seeing the worry on Mrs. Stafford's face, Marc added, "You know, Kim's the brightest girl I've ever met. That's one of the reasons why I care for her so much. I bet she's going to figure a way out of this. And we're all going to help her."

* * * * * * * * * * * * * * * * * * * *

Mercy Hospital
Intensive Care
Midnight

Dr. Ron Mackson shook his head sadly as he walked out of the curtained cubicle in Neuro Intensive Care. Officer Frank Elmo had just passed away.

At first glance, the head injury had not seemed that serious, but the examination in the hospital emergency room showed the sergeant to be in critical condition. Xrays revealed that the skull had been fractured by the blow. Apparently, Bernie had hit him with tremendous force. Massive brain swelling had occurred and despite the burr holes drilled by the neurosurgeon to relieve pressure inside the skull, Officer Elmo died three hours after the operation.

Dr. Mackson walked into the waiting room to tell Mrs. Elmo the sad news. A sheriff's deputy was waiting there with her, and she clung to his arm as the doctor told her of her husband's death.

They talked for awhile, and then the deputy asked Dr. Mackson if he would call the Multnomah County Sheriff's Office and report the death. Dr. Mackson put his arm around Mrs. Elmo briefly and then left to make the call.

Within minutes of Dr. Mackson's call, radio communications between law enforcement agencies in the state crackled with the new information. The Willamette Valley Gang was now wanted for murder as well as kidnapping and bank robbery.

* * * * * * * * * * * * * * * * * *

At the same time that Dr. Mackson was talking to the sheriff's office, another physician, Dr. Charles Wilson, a thoracic surgeon in Mercy Hospital, was having a conversation with Lt. Fred Blaine of the Portland City Police.

"Dr. Wilson, can you give us an idea of the extent of the wounded bank robber's condition?"

"Well, Willy Steimer is 25 years old. He received a gunshot wound to the chest. The bullet entered the front of his chest, pierced his left lung, just missed his heart, and lodged in a rib behind his lungs. What is it exactly that you want to know?" the doctor questioned.

"We're trying to determine the exact nature of the hostage situation that the abducted girl is in," Lt. Blaine explained. "If the young man dies, she may be in more danger than if he is kept alive."

"I see," Dr. Wilson said, rubbing his forehead. "That's hard to determine. He was a very sick patient. His lung was deflated, of course, due to the hole. We put a chest tube in and had just removed that the morning before his friends took him out of here. The lung should stay re-inflated naturally — he does have three shattered ribs, but I'd say his greatest danger is from infection. We had him on massive antibiotics — those stopped when the intravenous lines were cut. So if you're asking me if he's going to die — I'd say yes, but maybe not right away. He'll probably get sicker and sicker. Of course, if he gets rough handling, no telling what could happen. The rib where we removed the bullet was badly broken. If he moves too much, one of the broken ends of the rib could puncture his lung."

"Thank you, doctor; you've told me what I need to know," the lieutenant said. "Oh, one more thing. Supposing the abducted girl is put in a position where she has to take care of the man. Is there much she can do?"

"If she has basic first aid training, she may be able to prop him up and make him a little more comfortable. I'd say that would be a pretty hard position to be in — I certainly wouldn't want my life depending on his condition — no way!" the doctor said.

* * * * * * * * * * * * * * * * * *

Kim Stafford's house
2 a.m.

Marc stared at the packet traffic on the computer screen. Messages were coming in from net control operators all over the state. Monitoring schedules had been divided up so that each county would be adequately covered by listening hams. So far, no one had heard anything.

Mrs. Stafford knocked softly on the door. Marc turned and saw her standing with Sam, AF7S. He must have driven down from Portland.

"Hi, Marc, thought you might like a little rest," Sam said.

Marc started to protest, but Sam eased him aside and sat down at the computer.

"There will be someone else coming at 6 a.m. to relieve me — you can't do this thing all alone, so don't argue. Just go get some sleep. I'll wake you up if anything comes in."

"My husband is already asleep or at least he's pretending," Mrs. Stafford said. "I'm going to try to get some rest, too. Why don't you use the bed in the guest room — it's all made up."

Reluctantly, Marc followed her down the hall. He climbed into the single bed in the guest room and lay staring out the window. He doubted he could sleep.

Chapter 9

Christmas

December 25th — 10 a.m.
The cabin

T he sound of footsteps above her brought Kim slowly awake. She had been dreaming she was at home, and that she heard her mother getting up to put the Christmas turkey in the oven. Soon it would be time to get up and open presents.

Kim stretched and rolled over. Her shoulders were cold, and there was an unpleasant damp odor that made her nose wrinkle in disgust. Kim opened her eyes and reality hit her like a truck. The terror of the previous night raced through her mind as she rubbed her eyes, trying to become accustomed to the dim light.

Kim's right hand was numb from clutching her two-meter rig all night. How long had she lain awake trying to find a repeater? She couldn't remember when she had given up, but obviously, she had. *I hope my batteries aren't completely dead*, Kim thought. Gratefully, she noted that she had turned off the power before falling asleep. She turned the switch on and was greeted by the reassuring rush of static. She switched it back off and tucked the transceiver down in the foot of the sleeping bag along with the spare battery pack.

She hadn't been able to reach a repeater, but she knew that the small black transceiver was her main hope of survival. Silently, she set her mind to working on some sort of plan. Marc's miraculous survival in the Jefferson Wilderness last spring had taught her that the brain was a person's most important tool in conquering the insurmountable. *I'll think of something*, she told herself.

The men were up. She could hear their low voices rumbling. Kim squinted at her wristwatch. 10 a.m. It must have been 4 or 5 in the morning when she had fallen asleep.

The sunlight filtering in through the window slot made it possible for the first time to see the filthy room that was her prison. Cobwebs dripped from the low ceiling, and the floor was coated with thick dusty grime. Kim reached out and touched the damp cement wall next to her and then quickly pulled her hand back into the warmth of the sleeping bag.

It was tempting just to lie there, but she decided to get up and use the makeshift bathroom before the men came down to get her, as she assumed they would. As she put her feet on the cold floor, dust swirled and danced in the shaft of sunlight. Kim grimaced as she stood up straight. Every bone and muscle in her body ached. She hadn't been this sore since the first day of skiing season before Thanksgiving. Her bumpy ride on the cold floor of the van had taken its toll. Also, it hadn't helped to be shoved and grabbed the way she had been. She rubbed a sore place on her right upper arm.

Kim pulled aside the flimsy curtain and stepped into the closet bathroom. The porcelain sink was repulsive, but she turned on the water and splashed it on her face. The cold sent aching chills through her. There was no towel, so she dried her face and hands on the sleeve of a flannel shirt hanging on a peg. *Maybe I should be glad there's no mirror,* Kim thought, rubbing her eyes.

She put her white nurse's shoes back on and tucked the flannel shirt she had found last night into the waistband of the khaki pants. Everything was too big for her, but by turning the waistband of the pants over once, she took up enough of the slack material to keep them up.

Someone was thundering down the stairs. Kim ran her fingers through her tangled hair and stepped back into the room.

"Well, good morning, Nursie, or should I say 'Merry Christmas?' " It was Bernie and his voice dripped with sarcasm.

I wonder why he hates me so? Kim thought. She stared at him and tried to project an assertiveness she didn't feel.

"Boss wants you — move it!" he said gesturing toward the doorway.

Kim moved up the stairs quickly. Bernie had left the door open, and she hurried into the living room. Joe had his back to her as he bent over the woodstove shoving kindling into it. Sheila was awake, Joe's coat pulled tight around her. She met Kim's gaze with an angry glare.

"How's your arm?" Kim asked quietly.

Sheila ignored her, turning her head sideways to look at Joe. At the sound of Kim's voice, Joe stood up and turned to face her. He looked her up and down, obviously noting the pants and shirt from the closet.

"Good," he said. "I'm glad you found those. Now, go fix us something to eat."

"There isn't much out there — just some chili and peaches," Kim said. "Is that what you want?"

"Yeah, anything," Joe said.

"I'm hungry," Sheila whined. "It's Christmas, Joe. Couldn't you go get some take-out turkey dinners or something?"

Joe patted Sheila on the head and walked away. Kim watched as he went to sit on the stool by Willy, who appeared to be sleeping peacefully. She returned to the kitchen and picked up two cans of chili. She opened them and poured the contents into a large sauce pan.

Willy was starting to whimper as he woke up. Kim went to the doorway and watched as Joe bent over him.

"It hurts, Joe," Willy whispered. "I feel like something's sticking into my lung — I can't breathe very good."

Joe pulled the cushion behind Willy up a little more so that his chest was elevated.

"Better?" he asked.

"A little," Willy said.

Kim walked over to Willy's side.

"Could you eat something?" she asked. "Some soup or chili?"

Willy made a face and moved his head slightly.

"My stomach hurts. I hurt all over. Just wish I could drink something cold, like apple juice," he said.

Kim disappeared into the kitchen. She grabbed the can of peaches, opened them, and poured the juice off into a glass she found in the back of the cupboard. The juice filled the glass halfway, and she added ice cold water from the well to it. She poured a small amount of the mixture into a cup and carried it to Willy.

"Try this," she said, holding the cup to his lips.

He took a small sip. "Good," he said. He took a few more sips and then laid his head back on the cushion.

Kim took the peach juice back in the kitchen and put it on the counter to save for Willy. Joe appeared in the doorway.

"What was that you gave him?" he questioned her.

"Some diluted peach juice," Kim said. "If you don't get some sugar into him, he'll die for sure. He's probably going to die anyway, unless you get him to a hospital."

"It'll be too bad for you, Nursie, if he does," Joe said.

Kim tried to ignore him as he stood in the doorway watching her stir the chili. She held up the can of green beans.

"You want these, too?"

"Sure," Joe said. "Might as well make a real Christmas dinner out of it," he added bitterly.

Kim opened all of the cupboards one by one, looking in vain for some more food. There was nothing.

"So what are you going to eat after today?" she questioned Joe.

"Listen, Nursie, your job is to take care of Willy — not to worry about how we eat. Understand?"

Kim just stared at him. After a minute or so, he walked back and sat down by Willy. Now, Sheila started up again too.

"I heard what she said, Joe," said Sheila, getting up from her chair.

She walked into the kitchen and looked at the cans on the counter.

"Is this all we got?" she asked Kim.

Kim nodded.

"We're gonna starve, Joe, if we don't go to a store. Why don't we all get in the van and head for California. We can pick up some McDonald's for lunch."

Bernie shook his head and laughed.

"They don't serve McDonald's in jail, and that's where we'll be if we hit the main road in that van," Bernie said.

"Well, what are we going to do, then?" Sheila wailed.

"Just relax, Sheila," Joe said. "Let's just eat our dinner here and then we'll make some plans."

Kim served the chili and green beans on cracked plastic plates she found behind the cups. She matter-of-factly divided the food into four portions: plates for Joe, Bernie, Sheila, and one for herself.

"What makes you think you get something to eat, girl?" Sheila said angrily as she spied Kim's plate on the counter.

"Go ahead, eat it," Joe told Kim gruffly.

Kim stayed in the kitchen and ate the food quickly while the other three talked in the living room. They were discussing the food and money situation angrily.

"We either leave for California tomorrow, or we get more supplies to stay here," Bernie said.

"I wanna go to California," Sheila said in her childish whine. "It's cold here — can't we go, Joe?"

There was silence for a few minutes. Then Joe called to Kim.

"Can he travel?" Joe said, pointing to Willy.

"Well, you know she's going to say he can't," said Sheila. "No reason for her to want to leave here."

Joe reached out and grabbed Kim's wrist. She winced at his rough grasp and, seeing the expression on her face, he loosened his grip slightly.

"Nursie, supposin' when Willy is well enough to travel, we leave you behind here?" Joe said.

Bernie coughed in contempt, but Joe continued.

"But if you lie to us and tell us he's well enough to leave, and he's not, well then something very bad could happen to you," Joe said.

He started to say more but then shut his mouth and just looked at Kim. She pulled her wrist away from him and stood rubbing it with her other hand. Her thoughts raced. What were they planning on doing? Tying her up and driving off with Willy? She knew if Bernie had his way, they'd shoot her. Should she lie and see if she could get them to leave? She had no idea what answer would better her odds. She chose her words carefully.

"The only answer I can give you about your brother is an honest one. I'm not a nurse even though you call me one. I've only had some first aid training, but I can tell he's badly hurt. I suspect from how hot he feels that maybe he's running a fever. He may have an infection from the surgery. I don't know if he'll live, even if you were to take him to a hospital right now, but I'm reasonably sure he won't if you start driving long distances with him."

Everyone was staring at her. Kim closed her mouth after her lengthy speech and held eye contact with Joe. Finally, he looked away. Willy opened his eyes and looked right at Kim.

"Could I have some more of that juice stuff, please," he asked softly.

"Sure, Willy," Kim answered and went to the kitchen to get the glass. Again, she marveled at the difference in the three men. Willy was actually polite — how on earth did he get involved in this mess? She poured some of the juice into a cup and chopped a half peach into it. She came back with the cup and a spoon.

"Willy, could you eat a couple of bites of peach?" she asked.

"I'll try," he said.

Kim cut the peach into even smaller pieces and held one on a spoon to his mouth. Willy let her spoon it into his mouth. He chewed the peach slowly and swallowed. Joe watched her feeding Willy for a few minutes, and then, content that she was caring for him properly, he went outside to get some more firewood. Bernie disappeared into the bathroom, and Sheila seemed to be asleep once again. Kim looked around the cabin anxiously. If only she knew where Joe was, she might make a break for it. She hesitated. Willy caught her glance at the front door.

"Don't," he whispered. "Joe will shoot you."

Kim turned in amazement to face him. She raised her eyebrows questioningly. Was Willy actually trying to help her? She bent her head forward so Willy could whisper to her.

"I'm sorry," he said, barely audible. "I'm sorry I got mixed up in this — sorry you did too."

"How did you?" asked Kim, genuinely curious.

"No job, kicked out of Army. Then my big brother said he had a job for me. Should have known better, but I didn't . . ." His halting voice trailed off and he closed his eyes.

Kim straightened up as Joe came back in the door, his arms laden with fir branches. He banged the door on the cast iron woodstove loudly as he attempted to push the last of the wood inside. Sheila woke up and immediately starting griping.

"My arm hurts and I'm co - old!"

Kim looked over at her. Sheila's face was flushed and her eyes looked unnaturally bright. I bet she has a fever, Kim thought.

"Look at him — he looks okay," Sheila said pointing at Willy. "Let's get rid of the girl and take Willy and head to California. Boy, I can see those beaches now — hear that surf and feel the warm sand between my toes."

Kim swallowed hard. Here was Sheila discussing travel plans and Kim's death in the same breath as if getting rid of the girl was as unimportant as taking a taxi to the airport.

Joe came over and stood by Willy. Willy must have sensed his presence because he opened his eyes.

"How about it, little brother — feel like traveling?"

"Whatever you say, Joe," Willy answered weakly.

Kim shook her head in disgust as Joe put his arms under Willy's shoulders and hoisted him into a sitting position.

"What are you doing?" Bernie snapped. "We need a new van before we can hit the road."

"I know, I know," Joe said. "Just relax. I just want to see if Willy is up to making the trip."

Willy was gritting his teeth grimly, but a loud moan — almost a scream, escaped his lips and he fell limp in Joe's arms. Joe laid him back on the couch. Kim stared at the bright red patch of blood seeping through the front of Willy's gown.

Joe's and Kim's eyes met.

"The rest of my Candystriper skirt is downstairs on the bed. Go get it and I'll rebandage him," Kim said quietly. Then she added, "No telling how much damage you've done to him this time."

Joe left the room and came back with the skirt which he handed to Kim. She tore it into pieces and made a heavier pressure bandage than before. She pulled Willy's gown away from his bleeding chest and untied the towel strips holding the bandage made from her skirt in place. Kim gasped. Another one of the sutures had pulled loose. Now the open hole was even bigger and bleeding more freely.

"If you keep moving him around like that, he's going to bleed to death," Kim said, her voice quivering with anger.

She carefully let the towels strips lie where they were so that Willy wouldn't have to be lifted again. She folded and refolded all of the skirt material into a hard, dense pad and laid it against the gaping wound.

"Hold this flat to his chest," she told Joe.

He put his big hand on top of the material while Kim tied the strips back into place as tightly as she could. The blood immediately seeped through the patch but then slowed so that the circle of red didn't get any larger.

"We're staying here," Joe said matter-of-factly. "Tomorrow, we're going into town and buying some food and some medical supplies."

Bernie and Sheila were quiet. Bernie reached in his pocket and pulled out a cigarette.

Joe raised his foot and kicked it out of his hand.

"And another thing," Joe said angrily. "It's hard for my brother to breathe, so do your blasted smoking outside."

Bernie growled something unintelligible and bent to pick up the unlit cigarette. He got to his feet and went out the front door, slamming it behind him.

Kim got some cool water and sat bathing Willy's forehead, which was glistening with sweat. Her own head ached, and it was all she could do to keep her hands from shaking. Suddenly, she had the beginning of an idea that might help her. If only she could get back down to the basement to think about it alone!

Christmas Day dragged by slowly. Willy came in and out of consciousness. Kim sat by his side, offering him drinks of fruit juice and water every time he woke. Around sundown, Joe told her to fix the remaining chili and beans for dinner while he sat with Willy.

Bernie and Sheila were mostly silent except for the usual complaints from Sheila about being cold and wanting take-out food. At last, after they had eaten and Kim had tried to wash the cracked dishes in the cold water, she went to Joe and asked if she could go to bed.

"I'm tired," she said simply.

Joe looked at her and then said, "Stay here."

She heard him thumping down the stairs to the basement. He came back carrying the mildewed sleeping bag.

"Willy may need you during the night. Sleep here on the floor by him," he said, throwing the bag on the floor.

Kim reached a hand out and caught the bag before it touched the floor. If they heard her transceiver clunk against the wood, it would all be over. Silently, she spread the sleeping bag out and crawled into it. She could feel the hard metal of her two-meter rig against her foot. The men had their backs to her so she quickly grabbed the rig and slipped it into one of the deep pockets of her pants.

Was she ever going to have a chance to transmit? Kim felt despair rising in her. She turned on her side in the sleeping bag and closed her eyes, but tears rolled down her cheeks.

Chapter 10

Supplies

From Waldport to Reedsport
December 26th — 9 a.m.

K im put her arm over her eyes and tried to sleep. What little rest she had gotten was fitful. Willy had been feverish most of the night, and each time he whispered her name, she'd gotten up and bathed his face with cool water. He was no longer sweating; instead, his skin felt hot and dry. Kim knew that meant that he was getting dehydrated. She'd tried to make him drink some water or peach juice, but he didn't want any. About an hour ago, just at sunrise, he'd finally drifted off into a more peaceful sleep. Kim desperately wanted to do the same, but Sheila was awake.

"I'm hungry!" Sheila announced to the cabin.

"Shut up," snarled Bernie and rolled back over in his sleeping bag.

"Joe, I'm hungry!" Sheila persisted.

Joe got up and patiently went into the kitchen. He came back with the open can of peaches.

"Here," he said, shoving them at Sheila.

"Those are for Willy," Kim said quietly.

"Who cares?" said Sheila, gulping them down as Bernie laughed.

"There's another can," said Joe. "Besides, we're going to get some supplies today."

"Yeah, sure," said Bernie. "And if anyone recognizes us, they'll comb this area like river miners sifting for gold. What we need to be doing is heading south to California — should have done that last night."

Joe ignored Bernie. Instead, he looked at Kim and spoke gruffly.

"Go downstairs and get yourself ready. We're going to take a little ride to get supplies. Stay down there until I call you — we need to have a private talk up here."

Kim stood up and folded her sleeping bag. She took it down the stairs with her. If they were still here tonight, *and if she were still alive!* she hoped she would be allowed to sleep in the basement where she might have some time alone to try transmitting. She went down the stairs quickly, looking over her shoulder to see if the men were watching. No one was in sight so she flattened herself against the wall and tried to listen. Only an occasional word was intelligible to her.

" . . . do it, tonight," Bernie said loudly.

"I'll second that motion," Sheila said.

"No, not yet," she heard Joe reply. Then there was the sound of footsteps as someone walked across the floor. Kim slipped into the room and left the basement door just slightly ajar so that a little light from the stairwell illuminated the room. She heard footsteps come partway down the stairs and then return upstairs.

The arguing started again, punctuated with Sheila's high whines. Kim went into the closet bathroom and tried to wash her face and hands the best she could. There was no towel so she used the one remaining shirt on a hanger to dry herself. As an afterthought, she put it on over the clothing she was already wearing for added warmth.

She had just pulled her transceiver out of her pocket when she heard footsteps again, only this time they were pounding down the stairs. She shoved the transceiver back in her pocket just as Bernie came into the room. She patted her pant leg to make sure that the bulge of the small transceiver wasn't obvious. She decided it was worth the risk of discovery to take it along wherever they were going in the van.

"Come on, Nursie. Going for a little ride," Bernie said.

"My name's not Nursie — it's Kim," she protested.

"Sure, Nursie, come on."

He grabbed her roughly and shoved her up the stairs. Kim sensed a new violence in him. Whatever had been discussed in the living room hadn't been to his liking.

Joe was standing by the front door with two dirty rags in his hand. He reached out to grab her hands but stopped as Willy called out weakly. Joe grabbed Kim's arm and took her with him over to Willy's couch.

Willy's eyes looked bright with fever. His cheeks were flushed and he was struggling with each breath. He looked up at Kim and said, "thirsty," weakly.

"Sheila, get Willy something to drink," Joe ordered. He pushed Kim back out of Willy's sight and swiftly tied one of the rags around her hands and used the other as a blindfold.

"I don't know how to take care of a sick person," Sheila grumbled, but Kim heard her running water in the kitchen.

"Well, you'd better figure it out," Joe warned. "And if anything happens to him . . ." he left the sentence unfinished.

"Will you remember the grape soda and barbecue chips, Joe?" Sheila begged.

Joe slammed the front door behind them as he took Kim's arm from Bernie and guided her along the path to the van. She stumbled several places, and Joe jerked her roughly to her feet. Kim shivered as the icy wind hit her. It was colder than it had been two days ago. Above the sound of the wind rustling in the trees, Kim heard the unmistakable sound of water rushing. They must be near a stream or river. She turned her head, trying to take in as much information about her surroundings as she could, but then someone opened the back of the van and pushed her into it.

Joe and Bernie were silent as they drove down the bumpy road. Kim huddled against the cold metal side of the van and tried vainly to loosen her tied wrists. When they reached the main road, they turned to the left, and Kim made a mental note that they were heading south. They drove on for more than an hour, stopping once while Bernie ran into a tavern to buy beer and more cigarettes. Now, Bernie's cigarette smoke filled the van. Joe rolled down a window.

"Man, you're polluting the place," Joe said.

Bernie laughed and Kim heard the click of his lighter as he lit another. Joe cursed and rolled the window down all the way. Kim inhaled the cold, damp, marine air. The smell of the ocean was associated in her mind with many happy childhood outings. Now, she was beginning to connect it with these terrible people who were holding her hostage. She took a deep breath and tried to stop trembling.

"Far enough for you?" Joe questioned Bernie.

"Yeah, I guess so," Bernie said. "Park it over there in the alley behind that grocery store."

The van crunched across a gravel lot and stopped. Joe reached over the seat and took Kim's blindfold off. She blinked to accustom her eyes to the light. The van was parked behind a grocery store in a deserted alley. Joe pulled his pistol out and showed it to her.

"We're going in this store, all three of us — understand? Bernie and I are going to be standing over by the magazines while you shop. If you so much as hint to the clerk that there's a problem, you're dead and he is, too. Understand?"

Kim maintained eye contact with Joe but refused to say anything.

"So what we want you to do, is buy groceries — buy some things that you think Willy can eat — soup, that sort of stuff. And get some food for the rest of us — enough for about two or three days. Get the medical supplies you need to patch Willy up, too. You understand?" Joe said, brandishing his gun again.

Kim just stared at him.

"You just remember that this gun is pointed at you the whole time," Joe told her.

He and Bernie came around to the back of the van and opened the door. Joe reached in and untied her hands. He grabbed her hand and shoved a one-hundred dollar bill into it.

"Come on," Joe said, gesturing toward the store.

Kim slid across the floor and put her feet down on the gra⁊el parking lot. She slipped the money into her pocket and rubbed her wrists which were red from being tied.

"Oh yeah, one more thing," Joe said, as they walked up to the small grocery store labeled "Al's Market." "Get some grape soda and barbecue chips."

Bernie snickered. The three of them went into the small grocery store which appeared to be empty. Kim looked around, trying to catch a glimpse of something that would tell her where they were. The odor of smoked fish and coffee filled the air.

"Can I help you?" asked a white-haired man rising to stand where he was restocking some low shelves in the center aisle.

Kim looked over at the magazine rack, where Bernie and Joe appeared to be browsing. Joe's eyes met hers and glared.

Bernie put his hand in his coat pocket.

"Uh, no," stammered Kim. "We just came to get some supplies."

"You live around here?" the man inquired pleasantly. "I don't remember seeing you before."

"Uh, no, just passing through," said Kim. *Help! please help me!* she screamed silently in her mind.

The clerk turned his back to her and went on with his work.

"Lousy weather we had for Christmas, wasn't it?" he said. "Nice to see it stop raining for a day or so, but I expect we'll get some more."

"Uh huh," Kim said, looking at the floor.

"Well, let me know if I can help you find anything," the store clerk said.

Kim didn't answer. She grabbed a small shopping cart near the front of the store and began walking down the aisles. She put about ten cans of soup in the cart and several large cans of fruit juice. The Gatorade caught her eye. That was what Willy needed — something to get his fluid, salt, and sugar levels back to normal. *What he really needs is a hospital,* she thought, but she added several quarts of Gatorade to the cart. On an impulse, she went to the baby food section. Maybe, Willy could eat some of that. She picked up some pureed fruit and small cans of apple juice.

Then she went back to the meat section and scooped up several packages of hamburger. On top of the meat counter, there was a pad and pencil for people filling out seafood orders to be smoked. Kim glanced furtively over her shoulder and reached to pick up the pencil. She dropped it as Bernie stepped to the end of the aisle and glared at her.

"Hurry up," he said.

Kim turned her back on him and continued down the aisles. Joe had said supplies for two days, but she didn't want them running out of food again. Everyone was nasty enough without being hungry too. She added a bag of potatoes and some vegetables to the cart and grabbed Sheila's chips and soda. *I hope you choke on them,* she thought to herself.

The first aid supplies the store carried were limited, but Kim found some cloth bandages and a bottle of hydrogen peroxide. None of the bandages really was big enough, so she put a few cotton dishcloths in the cart, too.

She wheeled the cart to the cash register.

"I'm ready," she called back to the clerk.

He got up slowly and came forward.

"You sure you don't live around here?" he asked. "You look familiar."

Kim gulped. Unaccustomed to lying, she felt her face flush as she groped for words. She could see Bernie and Joe in the corner staring at her.

"Nope, just visiting while my uncles over there do some Steelhead fishing," Kim said, flustered.

"Where are you staying?" the man asked cordially.

"Oh, just in a cabin," Kim said, "by a river," she added.

"The Umpqua? Smith?" he asked.

For a brief moment, anger flashed in Joe's eyes so furiously that Kim thought he might shoot both of them right there. But he half smiled and spoke to the clerk.

"It's just a stream — south of here — doesn't have a name," Joe said. He went back to reading his newspaper.

"Got a baby, have you?" the clerk continued. "You don't look old enough to have a baby."

"Oh, it's not hers," Joe interrupted. It's my wife's. That seemed to satisfy the man until he came to the peroxide and bandages.

"Somebody hurt?" he asked.

Kim looked at Joe, waiting for him to answer. He gave a barely perceptible nod at her, indicating she should answer.

"It's for my uncle's dog," Kim said quietly. "Ran into some barbed wire."

"Well, that's sure too bad — hope you can fix him up. We've got a right-good vet here in town if you need to bring the dog in."

Kim didn't say anything. The man seemed determined to comment on each item she was buying. He picked up one of the jars of Gatorade and smiled.

"Running in a marathon?"

"No . . . my uncles drink it while they're fishing," Kim said, stammering.

The clerk laughed.

"I'd think hot coffee would taste better in this weather," he said.

Just then Kim's eyes caught a glimpse of the stack of newspapers at the edge of the counter. "Reedsport Tribune — December 26th" the heading read, but it was the top headline that grabbed Kim's attention. "Bank Robbers Take Hostage."

Kim picked up a paper and turned it around so that the headline was facing the clerk. She put her hand beside the title so that her fingers were pointing right at the headline. The clerk wasn't looking.

"Oh, you want a paper, too?" He took the paper from her hand, folded it, and placed it in one of the grocery sacks.

Kim glanced out the window. The street was deserted. If she yelled, both she and the clerk would be dead, and Joe and Bernie would be gone before anyone knew what had happened.

"That'll be forty seven dollars and fifty one cents," the clerk said.

Kim handed him the one hundred dollar bill, trying to make eye contact.

"Whew," the man whistled. "Don't carry much small change, do you."

"I'm sorry," Kim said. "That's all I have."

"No problem," the clerk said cheerfully. He counted back the change to her.

Joe stepped up to the counter and grabbed the two heavy sacks.

"Having any luck with those Steelhead?" the clerk said.

Keeping his head down, Joe grumbled, "Not much. Come on N . . ." — he had started to say "Nursie" but changed it to "now."

Reluctantly, Kim walked out the door with him. Bernie put down the magazine he was reading and followed them.

The storekeeper stood scratching his head as he watched them walk past the store windows to the back parking lot. There was something really strange about those people — something really strange indeed. The girl had seemed almost frightened. Well, who wouldn't be with uncles like those two. They looked more like thugs. And if they wanted good Steelhead fishing, some of the best streams were directly north of them, not south. He shrugged and picked up the morning paper to take it back to the small kitchen in the rear of the store. Time for a coffee break.

It was a slow day in the grocery store. The girl and her "uncles" had been the only customers all morning. Probably wouldn't be many customers for hours, Al Davis, owner and chief clerk of Al's Market thought, as he poured himself a cup of strong black coffee from a pot on the small stove in the kitchen area. He poured some cream into the cup and then sat down with the paper in his lap. The usual headlines for their small town. Another mill had closed down on the coast. Unemployment was up; tourism was down. More rain forecast for the weekend. A sewage spill in Yaquina Bay had contaminated the shellfish. He paused. "Bank Robbery —."

Normally, Al ignored the lead stories, preferring to read the local news that really concerned him. But something made him scan through the story and then flip the paper open to page two. A girl's photo stared at him from the top of the page and Al stared back. That was the same girl who had just bought groceries!

He ran out into the parking lot and then walked cautiously around behind the store. Sure enough, there were fresh tire tracks in the mud and gravel. Al Davis scratched his head again. Hadn't the man said they were going south? Whatever vehicle had parked here had backed up and then headed north up the alley. Al went back into the store to call the Douglas County Sheriff.

Chapter 11

Clues

December 26th — Noon
Alsea Bay — Waldport, Oregon

N7FDF, Randy Michaels, climbed out of the cold water of Alsea Bay with a smile. His wife had laughed this morning when he said he couldn't wait another day to try out his new wetsuit she'd given him for Christmas.

"It's barely stopped raining," she said. "The water will be so murky you won't be able to see anything."

"Just plan on crab for dinner," he had told her as he happily piled all his gear in the back of their pickup. And he had made that same prediction to a few hams he talked to on two meters on the short drive from his home in Yachats to the Alsea Bay in Waldport.

Now, Randy admired the bulging bag of crab he held in his hand. Admittedly, it had been slow going in the bay, but he'd caught the incoming tide as the crabs were moving along the sandy floor up toward the bridge. His new wetsuit worked perfectly. After all those years of battling the various rips and holes in his old one, it was a pleasure to be comfortable as he dove for the wily Dungeness crustaceans. He'd found a huge cluster of them moving around the bridge pilings. He carefully measured the carapace of each male crab to make sure it was of legal size before stuffing it in his netbag. Within 45 minutes, he had his limit.

Randy had gathered enough driftwood for a beach fire before he ever got in the water. Now he lit the fire and sat down by the hot blaze to wait. The skies were almost clear today. Who knew? — they might even get sunshine for New Year's — certainly a rarity in Oregon. The fire settled down and Randy got his big steel kettle out of the back of the truck.

He filled it with seawater and put it on the fire. He quickly cleaned the crabs at the water's edge and plopped them into the boiling salty water. He could never understand why people cooked crabs before they cleaned them — kind of like cooking a whole cow intact, he thought. The crabs simmered, and when they were done to a perfect reddish glow, Randy drained the water and popped them into a waiting ice chest. He gnawed on one of the big succulent pincers as he carried his bounty to the truck. He could hardly wait to see his wife's expression. She was probably planning on turkey stew tonight.

He loaded up all his gear and drove back up through the Bayshore development to Hwy 101. He would just go across the bridge and stop in town to pick up some lemon juice and French bread — maybe a bottle of Riesling wine, too. There was hardly any traffic as he crossed the bridge and turned left on Hwy 34 to drive up to the main market.

Maybe they would put the kids to bed early and eat in front of the fire, Randy mused as he edged over to the middle of the street to turn left into the market. Suddenly, he jerked in his seat as a loud horn blared behind him. He looked in his rear view mirror as a gray van came barreling up on him and then swerved at the last minute to pass him on the right, just missing him by inches.

"What's your hurry, Mister!" Randy said aloud angrily. The guy must be going 90. Instinctively, Randy memorized the Oregon license plate of the van as it zoomed by: "KMR 322" and then jotted it down on the back of a gas receipt. A small gust of wind, wafting through the partially open window, caught the receipt, and it fell to the floor amidst the clutter of Randy's diving gear.

* * * * * * * * * * * * * * * * * *

December 26th — 1 p.m.
Reedsport

"And you're absolutely sure this is the girl?" Sgt. Skip Wallace of the Douglas County Sheriff's Department said as he held a photo of Kim Stafford out to Al Davis in his Reedsport grocery store.

"Absolutely," said Al. "She was a very pretty girl — I noticed that right away. Spitting image of her picture here except she looked kind of tired and her hair was all messed up. But lots of people come in here with messy hair. The wind, you know."

"And the other two guys?" questioned Sgt. Wallace.

"Well, they both wore coats so I couldn't guess how much they weighed, but one of them was about six feet, I'd guess, and the other guy a little shorter. I think they both had dark hair — seems like one of them had curly hair. I don't know. They both wore hats. I didn't really get that good a look at them," Al said. "Bank robbers, huh? whew . . ."

"Worse than that," Sgt. Wallace said. "They're wanted for murder."

Sgt. Wallace reached in his jacket pocket and pulled out mug shots of Joe Steimer and Bernie Knissen. He had wanted to hear Al Davis describe the suspects before he showed him the photos.

Al took one look.

"That's them all right," he said. "That poor girl," he added, shaking his head.

"Anything you can tell us may help. What kind of stuff did they buy?"

"Oh, lots of stuff — meat, baby food, Gatorade — I remember that. Well here, I can tell you exactly. This cash register makes a duplicate tape of the purchases."

Al opened the back of the register and took out the printed tape. He unwound it by hand and clipped off the segment that showed Kim's groceries. Sgt. Davis pored over it in detail.

"Peroxide, bandages — sounds like somebody's hurt, doesn't it?" the sergeant commented.

"She said it was for her dog," Al said.

"Yeah, sure," Sgt. Wallace said. "I suppose the baby food is for her dog, too?"

"No, she said that was for her aunt's baby," Al said as he and Sgt. Wallace both looked at each other in puzzlement.

"You know, I asked her about all this stuff, too — just trying to make conversation, but I could tell she didn't want to talk much. I thought maybe she was just shy."

"Can you think of anything that she might have said that would give a clue to where they were going?" the sergeant asked.

"Well, now that I think about it, that poor kid was probably trying to tell me something the whole time," Al said. "She said something about being in a cabin, and she added 'near a river' with quite a bit of emphasis. I asked her where it was, and one of those men stepped up and said 'south of here.' That struck me as funny because she said they were Steelhead fishing, and round here, most people think the best fishing is just directly north of here. That guy obviously wanted her to shut up. He picked up the groceries and they all went out the door," Al said.

The sergeant walked out into the parking lot with Al to inspect the tire tracks.

"You sure these are theirs?" Sgt. Davis asked.

"Well, just look at them," Al said. "This town's been so quiet, no one's driven out the back way since Christmas Eve. And then we had all that rain, so this is fresh mud today."

The two of them looked at the tire tracks. Sgt. Wallace bent down and examined the indentations where the vehicle had been parked. He paced off the distance between the front and rear wheels.

"About the right distance apart for a van," he said. "And you're right about the direction," he said looking up the alley — "looks like they headed north. You don't suppose they drove up the alley to the next street and then turned onto the main drag and came back, do you?" asked the sergeant.

"Why would they have bothered to do that when they could have just gone out the parking lot and turned right?" Al said.

"Good question," muttered Sgt. Wallace. He thanked Al Davis for the information and gave him his card with his phone number. Al handed him the cash register tape and jotted down his address and phone number on it. Then Al went back in the store. The second customer of the day had just come in.

Sgt. Wallace climbed back in his patrol car. He radioed his new information back to the station and said he was going to scout a few of the local roads. Before he started the car, he read over the register tape again. What an assortment of items! Baby food — that really puzzled him. Who would be eating baby food?

He pondered this question as he pulled back onto Highway 101 and headed north. Who would eat baby food other than a baby? Sgt. Wallace smiled as he remembered eating baby food himself, just two years ago.

"They don't come any worse than those," the oral surgeon had said after he had removed his impacted wisdom teeth. Sgt. Wallace believed him after the local anesthetic wore off. He had barely been able to open his jaws for two weeks. His wife had gotten the idea of buying baby food, and he had carefully spooned the pureed mixture into his painful mouth.

So that was one reason someone might eat baby food. What might another one be? Sgt. Wallace asked himself. One of the robbers was wounded — maybe he was too weak to chew. It was just speculation on his part, but the sergeant thought he would share his ideas with his captain once he got back to the station.

But first, he wanted to explore a few roads. He turned right from Highway 101 onto a logging road near Gardiner. The store owner had said one of the robbers had seemed startled when he mentioned Smith River. Well, he would just check out that area.

He drove along the road looking for cabins nestled in among the trees. There were a few but he didn't see any vans. Unless they were going to do a door to door search of the entire coast, they would just have to wait for some more clues. He drove back down the road to 101 and stopped in a few gas stations. Had anyone seen a van — perhaps traveling at high speed — go by? One young attendant thought maybe he had, but he wasn't sure. Sgt. Wallace shrugged. He was wasting time — better to get back to the station and see if anything else had developed in the case.

* *

December 26th — 3 p.m
Portland Police Station

Lt. Fred Blaine, of the Portland City Police, motioned for the other officers to come in and sit down. Among them were two FBI agents, three Multnomah County Sheriff's officers, and several officers from the Portland City Police, all assigned to the investigation.

"We're beginning to get some information in from the coast," Lt. Blaine told the officers. "A store owner in Reedsport believes the suspects came into his store this morning. They bought enough food to indicate they might be staying around for awhile. One of the suspects said they were heading south, but the store owner thinks they were going north. We have several Douglas County Sheriff's officers searching side roads within a ten mile radius of Reedsport now."

"Any word on the vehicle?" asked one of the FBI agents.

"No," said Lt. Blaine, "except that we believe it's a van of some sort."

For about an hour, the officers shared the information they had, including Lt. Blaine's conversation with Dr. Wilson at Mercy Hospital concerning Willy Steimer's condition and, of course, the earlier news that Officer Elmo had died.

"Has anyone figured out how much money these guys have?" one police officer asked.

Lt. Blaine spread some tally sheets from the various banks robbed over the last few weeks.

"Well, they dropped the whole bag when it blew up in that one robbery. In two others, they happened to stick up tellers who had just made vault deposits, so they only got a few hundred dollars. The one job in Corvallis was where they got the most — maybe five thousand and it was all in large bills. The vault teller stuffed the bag with dummy bundles — just paper with twenties showing on either side," said Lt. Blaine.

96

"You think they'll try another job?" one of the men asked.

"I don't know," said Lt. Blaine. "If they're going to leave the country — which is what I'd guess their plan would be — they're going to need more money. I'm sure they would be long gone by now if it weren't for the wounded man. He's probably so critical that they can't move him at all. The fact that they were buying groceries indicates they're holed up somewhere."

"And how does the abducted girl figure into all of this?" asked another officer.

"We're not sure," said Lt. Blaine. "If they just wanted a hostage to get clear of the hospital, they would have dumped her or killed her long ago. The fact that she's still alive must mean that they need her for something. Our best guess is that she's tending to the wounded man."

"And if he dies?" one of the FBI agents asked quietly.

Lt. Blaine shook his head.

* * * * * * * * * * * * * * * * * *

December 26th, 7 p.m.
Kim Stafford's House

Marc stared at the computer screen in front of him. The Lan-Link program allowed him to see incoming messages from many stations at once. At the moment, he had the ARES coordinators from Medford, Brookings, Astoria, and Coos Bay all on the screen. They were reporting that round the clock monitoring of the two-meter frequencies had not turned up a signal from Kim as yet.

Marc had just received a phone call from Lt. Baxter at Marion County Sheriff's Office, telling of the gang's believed appearance in the Reedsport area. Marc typed this new information on to the computer screen and directed it to all the coastal ARES people involved. Within minutes, the first of the acknowledgments came back from Lincoln City. "Situation understood — will keep monitoring."

Marc looked down at the Oregon map that Mr. Stafford had brought him from his car. Kim had one on the wall, but Marc wanted one that he could mark with a red felt tip pen.

He put a big circle around Reedsport and bent over the map closely to stare at the tiny inland roads leading to the coast highway.

He raised his head as he heard conversation in the living room. A moment later, Cliff Siddell, N7FLE, walked into the bedroom.

"What brings you up here from Corvallis?" Marc asked in surprise.

"Just want to help — that's all. I called your parents and they said you were here. From the looks of you, you could use a good night's sleep, too."

Marc didn't argue that point. He had been running the packet setup plus monitoring two-meters voice for the past eighteen hours. He stood up and rubbed his eyes.

"Well, okay," Marc said slowly, "but you better promise to holler if anything happens!"

"Agreed," said Cliff.

Marc made his way down the hall to the guest bedroom and collapsed on the bed. He was asleep before he had a chance to take off his shoes. Mrs. Stafford came to the doorway a half hour later, shook her head, and covered him up with a warm quilt.

Chapter 12

A Gift From Uncle Steve

December 26th 8 p.m.
In the Cabin

A t first, when the men and Kim had gotten back to the cabin, Kim had almost been able to forget her situation as she busied herself putting away the groceries. Willy was asleep, so the men left her alone as she tidied the kitchen. Among her purchases was a large bottle of soap. She squirted the fragrant liquid all over the grimy counters and sink and scrubbed away with one of the new dishcloths. The rest of the dishcloths she was saving as bandages for Willy.

Everyone was hungry. She could tell, from the temper exchanges she heard from the living room, that empty stomachs were making their normally bad dispositions even worse. Kim worked quickly as she browned some hamburger in a cast iron skillet and chopped up an onion with it. The aroma was enough to make her own stomach growl. None of them had really eaten anything since yesterday. She chopped some potatoes and carrots into the skillet, added a can of stewed tomatoes and some water, and then covered the pan with a rusty lid to let the stew simmer.

As the food smells permeated the small cabin, both Joe and Bernie came to the doorway.

"Man, when do we eat? My stomach's gnawing on my backbone," Bernie said.

Sheila was happily munching on her barbecue chips and drinking down a can of grape soda. *At least while she's eating, she doesn't complain so much,* Kim thought.

The men went back in the living room and sat down by the fire. Soon, the stew was ready, and Kim scooped it up into the cracked cups and carried it to them and Sheila. She stopped by Willy's couch to look at him. Red pinpoints of fever marked his flushed cheeks and he breathed with deep shuddering sighs as he slept. Kim got a wet cloth and bathed his face, but he didn't wake up. She dished up a cup of stew for herself and ate it standing in the kitchen. She had barely begun before Joe and Bernie were calling for more.

She wanted to tell them to get it themselves but quietly went into the living room and took their cups for refills. Bernie slurped down the second cup almost as fast as the first and then lit a cigarette. Kim stayed out of sight in the kitchen, but she could tell by his footsteps that he had gotten up and was now standing by the woodstove. He began swapping tales with Joe.

"Remember old man Hibbard in the cell next to mine?" Bernie laughed.

"Yeah, he'd break out in hives every time they served us carrots. And they served carrots every day," Joe chuckled.

"Always scratching, he was, that's for sure," Bernie said. "I asked him once why he ate the things if they made him itch. You know what he said? 'I like 'em.' Well they sure didn't like him."

"You should talk about itching!" Sheila taunted Bernie.

Bernie and Joe both laughed, but just then Willy woke up with a high pitched cry which startled everyone.

"Help me," he wailed.

Kim was at his side in a flash.

"What is it, Willy?" she asked.

"I can't breathe," he coughed, sputtering. "It hurts so bad." He coughed again and a small amount of blood stained the corners of his mouth.

His voice trailed off. Kim pulled the sleeping bag and his gown back. The bandages appeared to be okay — no new bleeding. He was so hot though that she could feel the heat from his body several inches away. She wondered if the coughing up blood meant he had pneumonia or some other kind of infection.

"How will it feel to be responsible for your own brother's death?" she said quietly, looking right at Joe.

Bernie leaped across the room and gave her a shove so hard that she fell to the floor. She looked up just in time to see Joe's big hands grab Bernie and whirl him around, pinning him against the wall.

"Leave her alone," Joe growled.

"You gonna take that kind of talk from her?" Bernie said.

"What's it to you — you don't care about Willy, anyway," Joe said.

"I don't like to see any half-pint girl sass a grown man," Bernie said.

Joe ignored him and turned his attention to Kim as she got up slowly from the floor.

"Keep my brother alive," he said simply and walked back over to the woodstove and sat down on the floor in front of it. Sheila leaned forward from the rocking chair and massaged his shoulders.

Kim went to the kitchen and poured some Gatorade into a cup. She brought it back to Willy.

"Drink this," she urged, holding it to his lips.

He took small sips, but, after three or four, he lay back exhausted. Kim bathed him with cool water and wiped his face with one of the clean, new cloths.

It had been dark for several hours. Sheila was yawning by the fire, and Willy eased back into a fitful sleep. Kim stood up and turned to Joe.

"I'm exhausted," she told him. "Please let me go downstairs and get a couple of hours of sleep. I can't sleep up here. If Willy needs me, just call me."

Joe was silent for a minute and then said, "Okay."

No one moved in the room and Kim hesitated. Finally, she walked across the floor. She could feel their eyes boring into her back as she left the room to go down the stairs.

At last! She was alone. She was tired — that was no lie, but she certainly didn't plan on sleeping. She had work to do! Actually the idea had come to her in the kitchen while she was cooking dinner. Something about the odor of the stew brought up mental pictures of her own mother cooking dinner, and she pictured them all sitting around the table without her.

Of course her Uncle Steve would be there. Whenever he was in the country, he joined them for holidays. This year, he had put an intriguing package under the tree for her. She had no idea what it was, but she was sure it had something to do with Amateur Radio. Last year, he had given her all sorts of reference books, and it was that memory that had given her an idea. One of the books had been the ARRL's *Antenna Book*. One of her uncle's specialties was antennas, and she had sketches he had drawn for a manual of his own. She had them pinned up around her bulletin board. The one that was right above her computer was something called a "J" antenna.

"Thank you, Uncle Steve," she whispered as she groped her way through the darkness to the bathroom. She tiptoed across the cold, clammy floor and felt along the wall until she came to the vinyl curtain covering the toilet and sink. Concentrating on not making a noise, she lifted off the top of the toilet tank and laid it across the sink. She plunged her hand into the icy water to retrieve the pair of surgical scissors she had hidden in the tank.

Footsteps and loud talking above startled her. Heart racing, she quietly put the tank top back in place. She dried her cold wet hand off on the baggy khaki pants and grabbed the scissors. Still feeling her way along the wall, she inched toward the antique rusty stove on the far wall. A miniscule shaft of moonlight from the window slot outlined the stove slightly. She crouched beside it.

Okay, so far, so good, Kim mentally whispered. Her hands were shaking from both cold and fear. Clumsily, she grasped the icy wet scissors and held them by the stovepipe. The metal was thin and rusted. Kim said a silent prayer as she plunged the tip of the blades into the metal on the backside of the pipe. If the men came down here in daylight, she couldn't have any visible evidence of what she had done. Her intrusion into the metal made a slight screeching noise, and Kim waited anxiously to see if anyone upstairs had heard her. Silence.

Wiggling the point of the scissors into the metal, she began to cut a strip about eighteen inches long and one inch

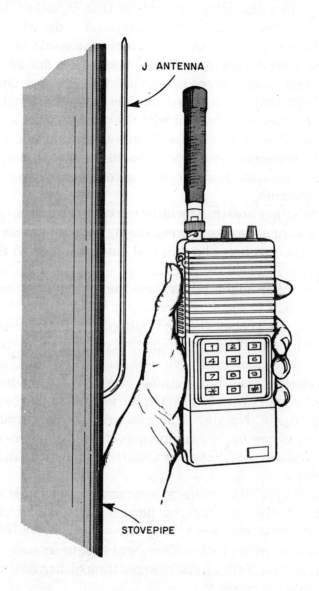

J ANTENNA

STOVEPIPE

wide from the pipe. The metal was so old and fragile that it cut easily, making very little noise.

Kim bent the strip upward so that it looked like a backward J. Now, what was she supposed to do? She didn't know of any way of hooking her rig to the makeshift antenna. Hadn't she read something about signals from one antenna transferring to another one in close proximity? In fact, she had a vague idea that was what a J antenna did — the signal from her transmitter should couple with the piece of metal, and the strip of metal would couple the signal with the main stovepipe. Since the stove pipe appeared to go all the way through the roof, the J antenna could possibly give Kim the effect of an outside antenna.

Holding her breath, Kim lifted her two-meter rig up about two inches from the J and turned the rig on. The familiar rush of static cheered her. She still had batteries. Now to find a repeater. She started the process over — the one that she had tried the other night of pushing the "up" button on the touchtone pad to move the frequency five kilohertz higher. Each time she pushed the "up" button, she also pushed the transmit button. If she had happened on a repeater station, there would be a melodic click — sort of a "kerchunk" sound of the repeater resetting. Nothing. She repeated the process over and over, moving up through the two-meter frequencies. Nothing. Again. Nothing. Kim pondered the mathematical possibility of how many combinations of numbers there were. She knew she was taking valuable battery time with this risky experiment.

"Kerchunk!" The noise of a repeater resetting startled Kim. Instantly, she pressed her mouth to the built in microphone and whispered "Help me — this is KA7SJP." She pushed the transmit button. There was a vague scratchy noise but no resetting noise. Despair surged through her. She wasn't getting into the repeater.

Desperately, she pushed the transmit button again and again. About every fifth time, the repeater would click, but when she tried to talk, she couldn't make the repeater hear her. She moved the transmitter a fraction of an inch closer to the "J" strip and tried again. "Kerchunk" It was loud this time. She listened for a minute — no one talking. Rather than risking valuable time trying to find a ham, she punched up "911" on the touchtone pad. Perhaps the repeater, wherever it was, had a link with the "911" emergency system.

"Lincoln County Sheriff's Department," a woman's voice answered.

"Help me, please help me," Kim spoke rapidly into the microphone. "My name is Kim Stafford, KA7SJP — I'm being held hostage by bank robbers."

"Do you know where you are?" the woman's voice asked.

"No," whispered Kim. "In a cabin near a stream about an hour north of Reedsport."

"Kim!" the shout came down the stairs, and Kim jumped. "Kim! hurry up — Willy's hurting bad."

Kim turned the rig off and stashed it under the stove as she heard thundering footsteps down the stairs.

Chapter 13

"Help me!"

December 26th 10 p.m.
911 Dispatch Center
Newport, Oregon

"**I**s he breathing? — What's your name? — Sally? — Okay, Sally. — Listen to me! Tilt the baby's head back gently. Now cover his mouth and nose with your mouth and just give him two little puffs of air. Did you do that? Good. He has a pulse, right? Okay — continue breathing for him. I'll count for you. One, one-thousand; two, one-thousand; b-r-e-a-t-h-e."

Linda Wetherly felt her own pulse quicken as she listened to Mary Eyers, her partner in the 911 Newport Dispatch Center, participate in this tense drama. Over the loudspeaker, she could hear the baby's mother making little sobbing noises in between the breaths she was using to force life back into her baby. Mary kept coaxing and instructing her.

"You're doing great, Sally. We have an ambulance on the way. Just keep breathing: One, one-thousand; two, one-thousand; b-r-e-a-t-h-e."

Suddenly, the weak cry of an infant punctuated the conversation.

"Oh thank you, God!" the mother cried openly into the phone.

"Sally? — you're doing fine. What's the baby look like now?"

"He's taking kind of gasping breaths and the blue color is going away."

Linda and Mary could now hear the wail of a siren approaching the house.

"Sally — listen. The ambulance is there. Wrap the baby in a blanket and take him with you to the door to let them in. I'll stay on the line."

"Okay," Sally said, still crying. "Oh thank you, so much — you saved my baby's life."

Mary and Linda sat silently, listening to the open phone line until a few minutes later when one of the paramedics reported that they were ready to transport the baby to the hospital.

"You did a great job, Mary," Linda said with honest praise.

"I feel shaky," admitted Mary. "It's been such a quiet night — that call kind of startled me."

It had been a slow night, but then most of their nights were slow, Linda thought. Since Mary was officially monitoring the phone lines this hour, Linda stretched and walked over to the window to gaze down on the dark vacant streets of Newport. In the daytime, rain or shine, the town was bustling with tourists who flocked to the coast to watch the whales, the storms, and other tourists. But tonight, the empty streets looked like a ghost town.

A light rain was falling, and the mist transformed the neon lights of the theater marquee into an iridescent glow. The one show of the evening would be let out in a few minutes. Linda wondered if anyone had bothered to attend.

"I guess I'll eat something — maybe it will settle my nerves," Linda said to Mary.

Mary nodded as she concentrated on filling out paperwork on the latest call. The two women were sitting in the small upstairs office 911 Dispatch Center over the Lincoln County Sheriff's Office in Newport. When the microwave dinged, Linda walked over to it and removed a steaming bowl of thick clam chowder. This chowder, for which the town was famous, always tasted good — especially on a cold night like this.

"There's plenty more for you, Mary, if you want some," Linda told her. "Kevin brought us a whole quart from the restaurant."

"In a few minutes when you're done — right now, I'm still coming down from the last call," Mary told her.

"That's the difference between us," Linda said, laughing. "You don't eat when you're nervous — I do. That probably explains why you're skinnier too!"

"Don't worry, Linda — I'll eat two bowls in just a bit," Mary assured her.

Linda glanced at the clock. Two more hours to go. Their shift was four until midnight. The next shift would arrive at eleven in order that they could be briefed on any situations going on. From eleven to midnight, there would be four of them in the office.

Then, at quitting time, Linda would drive up the winding road to her small frame house tucked in the hills above Yaquina Bay. It was lonely there, Linda reflected, but then peacefulness was what had attracted her to the coast. After ten years of working the night shift in Portland combined city/county Dispatch Center, and after a stormy divorce that had left her feeling emotionally shattered, she'd sought a place to unwind her coil-tight nerves. When her only child, Emily, started attending an out of state college last year, Linda sold their Portland home and moved to Newport.

What a change this job was from Portland! No gang murders, robberies, or hideous freeway traffic accidents. Instead, most of the nights were totally quiet. Except for an emergency like they had just participated in and the occasional heart attack victim, or even more rarely, a boating accident, most of the nights were monotonously silent. Plenty of time to reflect and sort out her thoughts.

11 p.m. — one hour to go. Linda finished the chowder and rinsed the bowl in the sink just as Dan Bass and Millie Schneider walked in the door.

They hung up their coats on the far wall and settled into chairs beside Mary.

"You take over while I brief them — okay, Linda?" Mary asked.

"Sure," Linda said, sitting down in front of the bank of phone lines and radios. She started filling out the routine end of shift paperwork while the others talked.

Br-r-ring! Linda jumped at the noise of the phone. Conversation between Mary and the relief crew stopped as they too listened. Linda grabbed a pencil and automatically jotted down the phone number flashing on the enhanced 911 screen. The enhanced system, allowing them to see the phone number of the caller, had just been installed a month ago. Already, they could credit it with saving two lives when the callers were too distraught to remember their own phone numbers and addresses.

Linda picked up her mike.

"Lincoln County 911 Dispatch — what is your emergency?" she answered.

"Help me, please help me," a quavering feminine voice said. "My name is Kim Stafford, KA7SJP — I'm being held hostage by bank robbers."

Instantly, Linda was alert. This was what she had been trained for, and the adrenaline surging through her body keyed her mind to ask the right questions. Bank robbers! The first thought that went through her mind was that this was a hoax, but something in the girl's voice convinced Linda that she was telling the truth. She scribbled down the girl's name and also the letters the girl had said after her name even though Linda knew the tape recorder was running.

"Do you know where you are?" Linda asked.

"Not really," the girl told her. "In a cabin near a stream about an hour north of Reedsport."

Just then, Linda heard a loud male voice shout "Kim" in the background and then the phone went dead. Quickly, she punched the phone number from the enhanced screen into the computer. Immediately, the information came back that the phone number belonged to an Amateur Radio repeater operating on the frequency 147.30 MHz.

"Hey," Linda said aloud in amazement. "Look at this. It wasn't a direct call. She was activating a repeater located in Newport. KA7SJP must be her Amateur Radio call letters."

Dan looked at the information on the screen and then walked over to the wall where a coastal map of Oregon was pinned.

"Puts her anywhere within a fifty mile radius of here," he said, drawing an imaginary circle with his finger.

Linda quickly dialed the 911 Area Supervisor and told her what had happened.

"She sounded sincere, she really did," Linda said. "I would guess it's the real thing."

"It is real," her supervisor told her. "We had a bulletin yesterday that law enforcement agencies are looking for a kidnapped girl somewhere near Reedsport. Broadcast your information, and, since Amateur Radio Operators are involved, give a call to the ARES (Amateur Radio Emergency Services) Coordinator, too."

Linda punched up various frequencies on her dispatch radio to contact the sheriff's department and other coastal police agencies. Next, she looked up the ARES phone number on her computer file and called the coordinator who told her that Amateur Radio operators would monitor that repeater frequency and others in the area continuously.

Within minutes of her broadcast to law enforcement agencies, Sgt. Kevin Baker thundered up the stairs from the sheriff's office below.

"Just heard your call, Linda. Could I hear a tape playback?"

There it was again — the quavering voice of an obviously frightened girl.

"I'm being held hostage by bank robbers!"

"When did all this happen?" Mary asked Sgt. Baker.

"Christmas Eve — she was abducted from a hospital in Portland by the Willamette Valley Gang when they sprung their buddy. They were spotted in Reedsport early this morning. That's where everyone has been searching all day — looks like they're near us here in Newport, instead."

He walked over to join Dan at the map while Mary made two copies of the tape for use by law enforcement officers.

"We'll start a sweep of the area immediately," Sgt. Baker said.

* * * * * * * * * * * * * * * * *

Midnight

Mary and Linda said goodnight to Millie and Dan and walked out to the parking lot together. The rain had stopped and for a moment, the moon was visible through a break in the clouds.

"Poor girl," Mary said quietly.

"That's for sure," Linda agreed. "I can't help but think of my Emily and wonder how she'd survive in a situation like that. Imagine what the girl's parents are going through."

* * * * * * * * * * * * * * * * *

Stafford Home
Salem — Midnight

"Torment" is the only word to describe what Kim's parents were experiencing. As the hours dragged on with no word from the police or sheriff's department, their anxiety grew. Every time the phone rang, one of them flew to answer it. It was usually a concerned relative checking in to see if they had heard anything.

At midnight on the 26th, the Staffords were sitting in the living room, staring at the flames in the fireplace. Marc was upstairs in Kim's room, watching the packet screen for any news. When the phone rang, he automatically reached over to her desk phone and picked it up.

It was John Alsance, AA6BC, ARES Coordinator for the mid-coastal region.

"I'm going to put the information on packet in just a minute, Marc," he told him, "but I wanted to call you directly. "Kim just called the Newport 911 line through a Newport repeater."

Kim's parents had picked up the downstairs phone, and he could hear their anxious breathing as John told the news.

"We still don't know where she is except that it's in range of the repeater. The entire search is being moved north, and I understand the FBI is on their way over here." Marc hung up so that Mr. and Mrs. Stafford could talk to John by themselves. In a minute, he went down to the living room to join them.

"At least she's still alive," Mrs. Stafford cried after her husband hung up the phone. "Oh my poor little girl!"

"I'm going over there," declared Marc. "Sam Mentor said he would come any hour of the night or day to take over for me here. I'm going to call him right now."

"But what can you do at the coast if you don't know where she is?" Mr. Stafford asked.

"I'm not sure," Marc admitted, "but I know I have to go. Maybe, she'll transmit on simplex and several of us who are near can triangulate on her signal. Or even if she comes through a repeater, we could zero in on the input frequency of the repeater. I don't know. I just know I'm going!"

The Staffords didn't argue with him. They had learned enough about Marc to know that he followed through with what he said he was going to do. True to his word, Sam Mentor was at their door in fifteen minutes. Mrs. Stafford gave Marc a thermos of hot coffee, and both she and her husband hugged him goodbye.

* * * * * * * * * * * * * * * * * * *

December 27th 1 a.m
Highway 20

The campus lights of Oregon State University glowed in the night as Marc drove past the outskirts of the campus on Highway 20. In just five days, the winter term would be starting. He and Kim, along with twenty thousand or so other students, were supposed to pick up their registration materials on January 2nd. He swallowed hard and concentrated on the road ahead of him.

His headlights bore into the darkness as he drove through the small town of Philomath with its sawmill right by the road. He made his way up the hill beyond the town and on through the coastal valleys. A deer scampered across the road and froze for just a second in the beam of Marc's headlights before running safely to the other side. Marc watched the deer's white tail vanish in the heavy underbrush.

Eddyville. The post office by the road. As he came into Toledo, just a few miles east of Newport, Marc switched his two- meter rig to the 147.30 frequency.

"KA7SJP from KA7ITR"

Silence. Then a minute later, several local hams came on the air and told him they were monitoring this repeater as well as other local repeaters for Kim. One of them invited Marc to stop by his house. Marc thanked him.

"No, I want to do some exploring. But thanks for the invitation. I may take you up on it later."

* * * * * * * * * * * * * * * * * *

December 27th, 1:30 a.m.
Between Corvallis and Newport

"Last place I want to go is Newport in the middle of the night," FBI agent Bob Beckham said to his partner, Louis Ramirez.

"Yeah, I know," Louis agreed. "When the boss called from Portland, I think I was just getting into my — what-do-you-call-it? My REM sleep — the time when you have all the dreams."

Bob laughed.

"Well don't dream now, Buddy. We've got a case to solve."

"Have you read the file on this one?" Louis asked.

"Yeah, the stuff came to me yesterday. Some of the jobs that gang has tried to pull have been jokes, but the kind of stuff they're doing now is certainly no joke," Bob said.

"Murder, robbery, kidnapping . . ." Louis whistled through his teeth. "If they ever catch these jokers, they won't be going on any coastal trips for a long time."

"Amen to that," Bob agreed.

"Hey, look at that," Louis said.

"What?" Bob asked.

"That barn — the one that says "DMSO — $18 a pint Last time I drove over here was probably four years ago. It used to say 'Jesus Saves' on that barn."

"The times they are a-changing," Bob laughed.

* * * * * * * * * * * * * * * * * *

December 27th, 2 a.m.

Linda Wetherly rolled over and looked at the digital clock by her bed: 2 a.m. She couldn't sleep. Pulling a robe around herself, she walked over to the bedroom window looking down over Newport Bay. The marina Christmas lights twinkled, and she could see the silhouettes of ship masts decorated for the harbor Christmas show. It was the kind of scene that made postcards. Then she thought of Kim.

Somewhere in that cold darkness, there was a frightened girl being held hostage by brutal men. Linda shuddered.

"I'm pulling for you, Kim," she whispered.

Chapter 14

Looking for Answers

December 27th, 3 a.m.
Waldport

Marc headed directly for the Sheriff's office in Newport. Before leaving Salem, he had given Lt. Baxter a quick call, telling him where he was going.

"What exactly are you planning on doing, Marc?" Lt. Baxter asked.

"I'm not sure," Marc admitted. "Perhaps just drive around and monitor simplex on side roads."

There had been a moment's silence on the line. Marc could tell the lieutenant was not happy with his decision to leave Salem. But his tone of voice was friendly when he started talking again, suggesting that he check in with the sheriff's office in Newport once he got there. Marc agreed.

And now, here he was. Sgt. Neil Fisher greeted Marc at the front desk of the small office when he walked in. The sergeant looked at the two-meter rig in Marc's hand.

"I bet you're Marc Lawrence — Lt. Baxter called from Salem an hour ago."

He stood to shake Marc's hand.

"Come on in the back room here. I'll let you listen to the tape of the 911 call."

Marc perched on the edge of the stool as the sergeant played back Kim's distress call. The obvious fear and stress in Kim's voice raised his own tension level to a new high. He stood up and began pacing.

"Don't you have any idea where they are?" Marc asked, anxiously.

"You know as much as we do," the sergeant informed him patiently. "She's within the range of the Newport repeater —

117

that's all we know. And we guess she's somewhere near a stream or river from what she said on the tape and to the store clerk in Reedsport."

"What did she say in Reedsport? — no one told me exactly."

Sgt. Baker hesitated. Lt. Baxter had said it was okay to share information with this young man as the Amateur Radio operators were instrumental in the search. Still, he didn't want him to go out and try to rescue her by himself.

"She and one of the men with her said something about Steelhead fishing — that's all," the sergeant said.

Marc stood up, ready to leave.

"What are you planning to do, Marc?"

"I'm going to drive around on the roads near here and monitor simplex," Marc told him honestly. "If she can't break the repeater, she may try simplex and hope someone's close enough. If there's any chance that she comes on for just a minute, I want to hear her. When it's daylight, I think other hams are going to do the same thing — especially in areas where we don't have base stations already listening."

"And if you hear her?" the sergeant questioned.

"I'll call you — I promise," Marc said.

"Call us every hour, anyway, Marc, okay? We'd like to know where you are."

They shook hands and Marc left. There were two dark-suited men getting out of a green Dodge in the parking lot. They nodded to him as he passed them on the gravel path. It was 3:30 a.m. Marc got into his car, turned the heat up, and began driving through the quiet town of Newport. He turned down every side road that he saw.

It didn't take long for him to realize that many of the dirt roads led to logging areas that had long since been closed. After struggling to turn his Chevy around in a particularly muddy turnout, he decided to stick to the main road until dawn. He drove as far north as Depoe Bay and as far south as Yachats on Hwy 101, monitoring and occasionally calling to Kim. Silence.

At 5 a.m., he turned back to Newport and stopped at an all night restaurant. He bought a map of the Oregon coast at the cashier's booth and settled himself with a cup of hot chocolate at a table by the window. After spreading the map out on the table, he traced the blue lines of rivers and streams near Newport with his finger. He had fished in this area a few times with his father, but most of the places were just names on the map to him. The noisy chatter of some men just coming in the door caught his attention. They were dressed for fishing and were obviously in a jovial mood. He watched as they seated themselves at the counter.

"You reckon they'll be biting today, George?" one man asked.

"I don't know, Ken — I'm beginning to think the Steelhead are on Christmas vacation."

"If I saw the likes of us, standing on a riverbank, I'd take a vacation, too!" Ken chuckled.

Marc got up and took his map over to the counter.

"You two after Steelhead?" he queried.

"Sure are, son, although so far we haven't been any threat to them," the man named George laughed. "How about you?"

"Well, not exactly," Marc said, "but I would like to know where some of the good Steelhead streams are in this area."

George looked at him curiously but obligingly pointed out several streams where the elusive fish were thought to be.

"Do many people live up near those streams?" Marc asked.

"Well sure, there are cabins just about everywhere there's a stream. Say, you fixing to go fishing or house hunting, son?" Ken laughed.

"Both," Marc said solemnly.

And that's the truth, he told himself as he thanked the men, folded up his map, and walked back to leave a tip on his table. *I'm fishing for answers and looking for a house — a very special house!*

He paid for his hot chocolate and went back out to his car. The first hint of dawn was beginning to brighten the winter sky as Marc drove south out of Newport back down the coast highway to Waldport. There were two or three roads he explored along the way, but none of them seemed to be leading to the type of terrain where he felt the robbers would be. He drove up to the newly constructed Waldport bridge spanning Alsea Bay. A narrow dirt road leading down the hillside was barely visible by the beginning of the bridge. Marc slowed down and made the sharp turn off the highway. The road was steep and he shifted the car into low gear. There was a cement abutment at the bottom, directly under the bridge pilings.

Marc pulled his car to the side of the road, got out, and stretched. The bridge above him rumbled with every passing car and truck. Crabbing boats were making their way out into the protected bay, and Marc watched as people dropped crab traps overboard and marked their locations with colorful floats.

A dog barked from somewhere down the beach. Marc walked through the wet sand and rocks under the bridge to see what was hidden behind the rock cliff and shrubbery. As he came around the edge of the wild growth of Shore Pines and shrubs, he spotted a small brown frame house nearly camouflaged against the rock face below the highway embankment. Marc drew a deep breath and ducked behind a tree while he watched a thin wisp of smoke curl from the chimney.

The barking dog, a soaking wet Labrador Retriever, spotted Marc and came bounding joyfully down the beach to greet him. His wet tail thumped Marc hard in the legs, and when he shook, the salt water from his coat drenched Marc. He reached down and petted the enthusiastic dog.

"Shhh Boy," Marc told him.

Just then the front door of the house flew open and a booming voice called out: "Charlie! Here, Charlie!"

The dog wheeled and ran up the sand dune toward the house. Marc watched as a silver-haired man, smoking a pipe, stepped out the door and bent to greet his dog.

"Some bank robbers," Marc muttered to himself. "Glad I didn't call the sheriff on that one."

120

His statement about calling the sheriff reminded him that he had promised to check in every hour, so he dutifully went back to the car and punched up the sheriff's office on the autopatch.

He was cold from his trek on the beach and poured himself a cup of coffee from Mrs. Stafford's thermos. He would start driving as soon as his hands felt thawed. First, he would check in with the ARES Coordinator and also the hams who were monitoring the various frequencies.

* * * * * * * * * * * * * * * * * *

December 27th 8:30 a.m.
Waldport

Randy Michaels, N7FDF, climbed into his pickup truck to head for work. His four day holiday was over — if you could call it a holiday. Right in the middle of his planned romantic crab dinner in front of the fireplace last night, they had heard a dripping noise in the hall.

The roof was leaking. Randy's wife, Alice, ran to get plastic buckets to catch the increasingly steady flow of drops from the ceiling.

"I don't get this — it's not even raining right now," Randy said.

The two of them got flashlights, and Alice held the ladder while Randy crawled up in the narrow attic through a trap door in the closet. He inched his way across the insulation-covered boards until he came to a soaking mess in the corner near the eaves of the roof. Water that had gotten into the attic from the previous day's rainstorm had taken 24 hours to seep through the insulation and the ceiling below. They listened to the steady drip of water all night.

"We'll just have to hope it doesn't rain anymore until I get home tonight and get a look at the roof," Randy told his wife as he kissed her goodbye.

As he turned out of his driveway, he turned on his two-meter rig for the short drive. Maybe some of his buddies would offer him consolation. The 147.30 frequency was quiet.

Strange — usually there were several people chatting this time of morning.

"N7FDF monitoring," he announced. "Anybody around?"

His friend, Jeff, came back to him immediately.

"Guess you haven't heard, Randy. There's a girl being held hostage by bank robbers somewhere near here. She called 911 last night on this repeater. We're trying to stay off it as much as possible in case she tries again."

Bank robbers! Something clicked in Randy's brain, but he wasn't quite sure what it was. Jeff's next sentence allowed him to make the connection.

"They're believed to be traveling in some kind of van, but that's just speculation," Jeff said.

Randy felt like slamming on the brakes as he had an almost photographic recall of a gray van honking and then zooming past him in Waldport.

"Say, Jeff — you're not going to believe this, but I think I may have seen that van. A van just about ran me off the road yesterday near the market on Highway 34."

"You'd better call the sheriff," Jeff advised.

"That's what I aim to do," Randy said. "I'm pulling into work right now — I'll use the phone inside so as not to tie up the repeater. N7FDF clear."

* * * * * * * * * * * * * * * * * *

9:00 a.m.
Sheriff's office — Newport

"This is like musical chairs," FBI agent Bob Beckham complained as an Oregon State Police officer walked in the door to the cramped office and took the chair Agent Beckham had just vacated for thirty seconds to pour himself a cup of coffee.

"Oh was this yours?" the officer said, rising when he saw Beckham walking across the room.

"Forget it; I'm tired of sitting anyway," Beckham assured him.

Soon, half the room was filled with standing law enforcement officers as representatives of various coastal agencies poured into the room. Lt. Harry Blaine of Portland Police arrived a few minutes after nine.

"I have a personal interest in this one," he said. "One of our sheriff's officers, Frank Elmo, was killed by these jerks."

Lt. Harry Keller of the Lincoln County Sheriff's Department edged into the room.

"Sorry to keep everyone waiting, but I just had a very interesting phone call — very interesting indeed. A ham operator just called from Waldport — wanted to know if by any chance we were looking for guys in a gray Ford van. Seems he was nearly run off the road yesterday in Waldport by a gray van going east on 34. He even copied down the license plate 'KMR 322.'"

"Think those are our boys?" Agent Louis Ramirez asked.

"Very possibly — just ran a make on the van and it's stolen all right — disappeared on the 24th in Portland near Mercy Hospital."

"Okay," Lt. Keller said. "We're going to approach this situation with utmost caution. There's a girl being held hostage, and if her captors see us go driving in force down the road, it might end her chances. We'll make this the base of operations until we get further information. I want as many plain cars as I can get with the drivers dressed like fishermen, loggers, or whatever, just kind of looking around. Pretty soon, someone going's to see something."

"What should we put out for the Amateur Radio operators?" one of the dispatch officers asked.

"Just ask them to keep monitoring the frequencies — that's all. I don't want this license number on the air."

* * * * * * * * * * * * * * * * * *

9 a.m
Highway 34

Marc felt his heart hammering against his chest as he drove across the bridge into the quiet fishing town of

Waldport. Just minutes before, he'd heard Randy's call, talking about the suspect van. Before he could break into the conversation to ask questions, Randy had left the air. Jeff came back to Marc, but he couldn't provide any more information than what they had both just heard.

"N7FDF said he was calling the sheriff," Marc said aloud to himself. "So I guess I'm not breaking my promise to keep the sheriff informed if I don't call him just yet. Think I'll have a little 'look see' up the road, and if I spot anything, I'll call in then."

Marc rolled the window down a crack. Even though it was only forty degrees outside, he realized he was sweating with nervousness.

Chapter 15

Pete Sheffield KH6XM

December 27th 9:30 a.m.
Highway 101 — 1 Mile South of Waldport

"• • • • • •" Pete Sheffield, KH6XM, raised his hand in greeting as a car honked the familiar "h • • • • i • •" at him in Morse code.

"I wonder how he knew I'm a ham," Pete asked himself aloud. "I don't have call letter personalized plates since I'm in a rental car — must have spotted my 'mag mount' (portable magnetic mounted antenna)." He smiled a moment in admiration of the other driver's keen eyesight.

As both a veteran Air Force pilot and retired commercial airline pilot, Pete had more than a passing appreciation of perfect eyesight. Even now at age 63, he could pick out objects on the horizon that would be a blur to most men his age.

The other driver's greeting gave Pete a warm feeling of friendship — he was certainly glad he had squeezed the antenna into his suitcase. Actually, bringing his portable ham gear with him had been a last minute decision for Pete. The drive up the west coast from Los Angeles to the Olympic Peninsula was a vacation Pete and his wife, Phyllis, had been planning for over a year. But just two short months ago, Phyllis had died of a heart attack at their home on the island of Oahu. Grieving, Pete had said the vacation plans were out. His three children, all living in California had insisted he make the trip anyway. They kept at him until he finally agreed.

"Mom would want you to — you know that. Besides, we're looking forward to seeing you."

So Pete had flown over to Los Angeles, rented a car and made his way up the California coast, pausing for visits with his daughter in Santa Barbara, his older son in San Jose, and his younger son, his wife and their two children in Los Gatos. He had fully intended to catch a flight back home to Hawaii from San Francisco, but the lure of the open road and the scenic coastline of Oregon and Washington beckoned him to continue. On the Saturday morning his flight was supposed to leave, Pete called the airline and changed his reservation to a date two- weeks later.

For the first day going north above San Francisco, he was sure he had made the wrong decision. He was so terribly lonely that every hour was painful. Thank heavens for his two-meter rig. To keep his mind off his dismal mood, Pete talked to a number of hams all the way from Eureka to Coos Bay. They kept him company — kept him from thinking about the empty front seat beside him.

Last night, he'd felt almost happy, but this morning, the aching loneliness had returned in full force. Even though he wasn't hungry, he forced himself to eat breakfast in a small restaurant in Yachats, on the central Oregon coast, overlooking a beach where people were out flying kites even in the gray December weather. The waitress had explained that the small town was considered "the kite capitol" of the coast, and that virtually no kind of weather could keep people away from the joyful sport.

The brightly colored sailing kites in the sky brought back memories of Phyllis and the children when they often flew kites in a city park on weekends. They had all become kite fans — flown them just about everywhere the family had lived during his Air Force years. He and Phyllis had continued the hobby in Hawaii when they retired there three years ago.

He shook his head slightly to clear away the bittersweet memories. Automatically, his hand reached to turn on the two-meter rig. He had it set on the local repeater frequency, and as he turned it on, he hoped that maybe the ham in the other car would be calling him. Silence. He announced his own willingness to talk by saying, "KH6XM/portable seven mobile monitoring." Any Amateur Radio operator would know by his call and explanation that he was licensed in Hawaii but was traveling in "seven" country.

Pete announced his call a couple of times, but there was no response. Thinking maybe the other driver might have tried to call him on simplex, he switched the dial of his rig to 146.52 and tried calling him. Nothing. Oh well. The guy probably just honked at him and that was all. Pete reached his hand over to switch off the rig but pulled it back quickly as a weak feminine voice broke the air silence.

"Help me," the voice quavered. "Is anyone listening? Help me, please help me!"

In a flash, Pete had the microphone to his mouth.

"This is KH6XM near Waldport, Oregon — what's the problem?"

The girl's voice, muffled with tears, came back to him.

"Oh thank you — I didn't think anyone would ever hear me. I've been kidnapped by bank robbers. I know they're going to kill me."

Pete pulled his car abruptly off the road and concentrated on the conversation. Like Linda in the dispatch office, his first thought was that this could be a hoax, yet the fear in the voice was real.

"Are you a ham?" he questioned.

"Yes," the girl whispered. "I'm so scared, I forgot all about my call letters. I'm KA7SJP — name is Kim Stafford."

"Okay, Kim — just one quick question. What's V in Morse Code?"

"Ohh," Kim cried. "You don't believe me, do you? V is dit dit dit dah. Look, I have a general class license. I have a Kenwood TS430S at home, and I operate on 10, 15, and 20 meters. Oh, please believe me!"

Just then, Pete glanced down at the unread newspaper he had picked up on his way out of the restaurant in Yachats. A headline halfway down the page caught his eye: "Girl Held Hostage by Bank Gang."

"I do believe you, Kim. Tell me everything you can."

Her words came out in a rush between sobs.

"I'm in a cabin — that's all I know. I'm in the basement except when they take me upstairs. One of the men, Willy, is dying. They think I can save him — I know if he dies, they'll kill me!"

"Kim! Listen to me. Take a deep breath. Now think real hard — can you give me any clues as to where you are? I'm hearing you on simplex near Waldport, so you must be close."

"We drove to Reedsport one day and it took about an hour," Kim said. "They had me blindfolded the whole way."

"When you drove back — did they turn the car right or left off the main highway?"

"Right," Kim said. "And then we wound around a real curvey road and then turned right again — went over a little hill, I guess. I don't think this cabin is right on the road."

"Good girl, Kim. Do you know what kind of a car you rode in?"

"It's a gray van — I saw it the night they kidnapped me."

"Kim — are there any windows you can look out?"

"Just a little slot. I'm standing by it now."

"What do you see?"

"Just the ground — this basement is mostly below ground."

"Have you ever seen the outside?"

"Just the night they brought me in and just for a minute."

"Do you remember anything?"

"It's a beat-up looking cabin. Wait — I remember there's a big fir tree to the side of the cabin and the top is broken off — looks like it was struck by lightning. Oh no! They're coming down the stairs. I gotta go. Please help me!"

Even as experienced a veteran as he was, Pete felt the hair on the back of his neck tingling as he tried to contact Kim again.

"KA7SJP from KH6XM — are you there, Kim?"

The voice that came back to him was male, full of the same charged emotion he was feeling himself.

"This is KA7ITR — are you talking to SJP?"

"Trying to — who are you?"

"A friend of hers — name's Marc. I just turned simplex on and heard you calling her. Did you hear her?"

"Yeah, I heard her — she told me all about the kidnapping. Say, I need to relay this information to the sheriff or somebody. Can you stand by?"

"Please tell me where you are and I'll come meet you," Marc begged.

"Okay — just a minute. Let me look. I'm on 101 just a little south of Waldport — pulled off to the side of the road. I can see the town up ahead."

"There's a pizza place on the right side of the road. Could you meet me there in the parking lot?" Marc asked. "I'll be there in two minutes."

"Okay, Marc — see you there. KH6XM clear and monitoring."

"KA7ITR clear."

Pete drove into Waldport and parked in the gravel parking lot of the pizza place Marc had indicated. The restaurant was closed, but there was a pay phone out in the parking lot. Pete placed a call to the Lincoln County Sheriff's office and relayed the conversation he'd just heard. Just as he was hanging up, Marc's blue Chevy came roaring into the parking lot.

Pete appraised the tall slender young man as he got out of his car. He looked young but mature. The deep circles under his eyes accentuated the worry reflected in them. Pete reached out his hand to shake hands, and Marc responded with a quick firm grasp.

"Hi," said Pete. "I'm Pete Sheffield — motoring up this way on vacation when I heard the call. I just talked to someone in the sheriff's office — they asked me to stop by right away. I will, but actually, I told them everything I know."

"Tell me exactly what she said, please," asked Marc. "I only heard the last sentence."

"Okay, Marc — is that what you said your name was?"

"I'm sorry," said Marc, rubbing his forehead in frustration. "I'm so upset about all this, I'm not thinking straight. I'm Marc Lawrence — KA7ITR — I'm a really good friend of Kim's. Do you know what this is all about?"

"Well, I didn't at first, but I've found out," said Pete, pointing to the newspaper lying on his front seat. "Doesn't sound like a very good situation — that's for sure. Now, you asked me what Kim said. She said that she was being held hostage — obviously very scared — poor kid. I tried to find out more from her about where she is. She doesn't know exactly, but it's a right-hand road off 101 and then over some little hill, she said."

"Just a minute," Marc said as he turned and plucked a map lying on his dashboard.

"A right-hand turn? Let's see."

He spread the map out on the hood of Pete's car and traced the possibilities with his finger.

"If you're hearing her on simplex, it's got to be right here near the town."

"That's what I told her," agreed Pete. "She wasn't able to tell me anymore except that there's a fir tree with a broken top out in front of the cabin. She said it looked like it had been hit by lightning. I told all of that to the sheriff's office, so I imagine they'll be out searching the roads."

"That's what I aim to do, too," Marc said.

Pete looked at him and Marc stared back, meeting his eyes honestly.

"Son, I think this is really a police matter."

"Yeah, I know," Marc said impatiently, "and I've promised I'll call in if I find anything. I'm not going to do anything stupid — I just want to have a look."

Pete could tell by Marc's voice that there would be no dissuading him. He grabbed his hand-held rig from the seat of his rental car, closed the door, and locked it.

"Come on — you've got a better radio than I do — I'll go with you for one half hour exactly — then I'm going to the sheriff and I want you to come with me."

Marc was in the driver's seat in a flash.

"The way I see it," Marc explained, "is that maybe they're somewhere up the Alsea River. Yesterday, Kim was taken down to Reedsport by the robbers to a store. They made her buy supplies, and the store owner asked her where they were staying. She was quite emphatic that they were near a fishing stream. The Alsea's the biggest one near here, so let's try that first."

They drove through town and turned right at the sole stoplight.

"Why don't you keep your handheld on simplex, and I'll turn my rig back to the repeater, just in case," Marc suggested.

Pete nodded in agreement. He liked the way Marc was taking command. For the first time in two months, his thoughts were not on his own loneliness. He looked out the window at the passing scenery as they passed a market and a school and headed up the winding road into the woods.

Marc was staring ahead with the concentration of a fighter pilot. Pete looked at him and felt an immediate affection for this intense young man. If he was a friend of Kim's, she had a good friend, indeed!

They rounded a deep curve and Marc pulled over to the side of the road. A small brown frame house was barely visible through the thick stands of Douglas Fir and shore Pine.

"Looks like someone's home," Marc said quietly.

He pointed at the wispy trail of gray smoke coming from the stovepipe on top of the roof.

"No gray van, though," Pete observed, pointing at a beat-up Land Cruiser in the driveway.

Marc was starting to open his door.

"Hey, where do you think you're going?" Pete said, grabbing his arm.

"I'm going to go up to the door and pretend I'm a fisherman looking for an address — how about 145 Alsea Highway?"

Pete shook his head. He could imagine what the sheriff's office would think of a plan like this. Still, he understood Marc's desire to find Kim as quickly as possible.

"Look, Marc. You can't go up there. Supposing, these guys have your friend right there with them, and she says something — then you're both dead ducks. If anyone's going up to a door, it's me. I'm doing this above my better judgment, but I'll try this one house."

Marc sighed as Pete got out of the car. He watched anxiously as the muscular, gray-haired man walked up to the door and knocked. The door opened, but he couldn't see who was there as Pete's broad back blocked his view. Pete was gesturing up the road. In a few minutes, he raised his hand in farewell and turned and came back to the car.

"Are your bank robbers in their seventies?" Pete asked him. "A man and a woman — woman uses a cane?"

Marc whistled through his teeth in disgust.

"It's okay, Marc — you're not going to find out anything unless you ask But I don't think going up to doors is a good idea. Why don't we drive on up this road about five more miles — I think that would be the end of the simplex range. If we don't see anything, we'll just turn around and go back to the sheriff's office. I told him I'd be there within the hour."

Marc started the car. They drove in silence along the forest road. There were a few more houses and cabins, but most appeared to be vacant. Marc looked at his odometer. They had come 6.7 miles from the 101 turnoff. Pete was right. They ought to turn around. This might not be the right road, anyway. He turned into a jutted dirt road that allowed him turning space and put the car in reverse.

"Wait a minute," whispered Marc. "Didn't she say something about the cabin being over a hill?"

Pete guessed his thoughts.

"Pull the car up around that bend, there."

Marc eased his foot onto the gas pedal so as not to spin any gravel as he backed out of the road. He shifted into drive and went around the corner. A large ·clump of Shore Pines hanging out over the road provided perfect cover for the car.

"Now listen," Pete told him. "We're just going to take a peek over the hill — that's all. No going to the door, no heroics. You understand?"

Marc looked at the older man and nodded. He didn't know much about Pete, but it was obvious that he knew what he was doing.

Silently, the two men slipped from the car and crept up the embankment. Pete was a foot or two ahead of Marc, and suddenly he motioned to Marc to drop to the ground. On their stomachs, the two men crawled through the tangled vines and grasses to the edge of the trees.

Marc felt his heart hammering as he looked down the other side of the knoll. In a clearing, about 100 yards to their right, was a small brown cabin. Next to it was parked a gray van. Pete tapped Marc's shoulder and pointed upward. A huge old Douglas Fir stood as sentinel on the right side of the cabin. The symmetry of its lush green branches came to an abrupt halt about forty feet above the ground. The entire top of the tree was missing!

Chapter 16

We've Found You!

December 27th 10 a.m.
Bankrobber's Cabin — Waldport

K im hastily dropped her transceiver behind the stovepipe and stepped into the center of the room as Joe thrust open the door.

It had been an exhausting night — three times, Joe had come down to get her because Willy was moaning and breathing in strange little gasps. Kim had done all she could do to make him comfortable, but she felt that he was dying. He no longer roused to consciousness when she adjusted the pillows underneath him. She bathed his feverish face with cool water and moistened his tongue with a little water, but other than that, there was little she could do.

Along about dawn, his constant moaning and raspy breathing was obviously getting on the nerves of Sheila and Bernie. Sheila grumbled and shifted in the chair that she'd slept in the past two nights. Bernie grabbed a sleeping bag and announced he was going out to sleep in the van.

"You want to sit and watch the kid die, that's your business," he growled at Joe. "I say let's get out of here."

"Yeah, Joe," Sheila whined. "How 'bout taking care of me for a change?"

She rolled up her sleeve to show her swollen arm with angry red streaks on it to Joe. Joe sighed. Kim had never seen him sleep since they had arrived. The exhaustion was showing in his face. He got up and blocked the doorway, gun in hand.

"Stay in here until I come back," he ordered.

Grumbling, Bernie sat down by the fire while Joe went outside.

"What's he doing?" Sheila whined.

"Probably taking the distributor cap off the van — don't think he trusts me too much to stick around," Bernie chuckled in an ugly voice. "Looks like we all get to stick around here until Willy-boy dies."

Kim shuddered at the tone of his voice. Suddenly, Bernie noticed her.

"And little ol' nursie over there — well now, what are we going to do with her? Doesn't look like she's doing Willy much good so Joe probably won't fuss much if we get rid of her. Unless he decides that Sheila here is too much trouble and wants to trade her in for Kim."

At that comment, Sheila let loose with a string of swear words directed at Bernie. When Joe walked back in the door, carrying the distributor cap in his hand, Sheila was screaming hysterically. Kim huddled against Willy's bed, trying to make herself as small as possible.

"He said you're going to leave me behind!" Sheila yelled at him accusingly. "Said you're going to take that girl along instead."

Kim watched the flush of anger creep up Joe's neck. Slowly, he opened the door.

"Out!" he said to Bernie. "And don't come back in until you've got some sense in your head — if that's possible."

Bernie slammed the door behind him. Joe put his arm around Sheila and shoved her, not too gently, back in the chair.

"Shut up, Baby," he said gruffly. "Bernie doesn't know what he's talking about. I'm not going any place without you and Willy. Now cover up and let's all see if we can get some sleep."

"Go to bed for a couple of hours," he ordered Kim. Gratefully, she scurried down the stairs and slept fitfully until just a few minutes before ten when the sound of Willy's coughing awakened her. Grabbing her radio, she held it up to the J antenna on the stovepipe and tried to raise the repeater again. No luck. In desperation, she switched it to simplex and began the transmission which caught Pete Sheffield's attention. Joe's descent down the stairs had ended her call to Pete for help.

136

Now, as Joe shoved her up the stairs, she frantically prayed that Pete would be able to bring help to her. Her thoughts were interrupted as Bernie banged the front door coming back in.

"Oh good," Bernie said. "Nursie's up — she can fix us some breakfast. I'm starved! Make my eggs over easy."

"Not before she takes care of Willy, she can't," replied Joe angrily. "All you ever think about is yourself."

"Well someone has to — you sure don't care about anyone except that corpse in there," Bernie growled.

At the word "corpse," Joe lunged up the last two steps and smashed Bernie in the nose with his fist. Bernie spun around and collapsed on the floor, holding his bleeding nose with his right hand. He started to get up, but Joe had his gun drawn. Silently, Bernie pulled himself to his feet and disappeared into the bathroom.

Willy was coughing again; bright red flecks of blood spattered the pillow beside him. Kim went to his bedside and pushed the blanket further under his shoulders to elevate him more. For a brief second, he opened his eyes. They were bright blue with fever, and he blinked several times before focusing on Kim. He didn't say a word — just stared at her helplessly.

"Your brother's awake," Kim said softly to Joe.

Joe walked over to the bed and looked down at Willy. His face contorted with emotion as he looked at the still form of his younger brother.

"Hey there, Willy, how's it going?" he said.

Willy opened his mouth to reply but no words came out.

"We're going to get you to a doctor and get you all fixed up. Okay, Willy?"

Willy smiled wanly and then closed his eyes. Joe turned in desperation to Kim.

"Can't you do anything more?"

"Not without a hospital — he's burning up with fever. You can see that," she said accusingly. "He may need more surgery, antibiotics, the whole works — I just don't know."

"We can get antibiotics," Joe suggested. "There's a clinic in town — have to wait until dark, though."

Kim felt her fear displaced by anger. "Do you know how many kinds of antibiotics there are? What are you going to do — just steal a bunch and give them all to him and hope one of them works? Supposing he's allergic to them — supposing that's not even what he needs? If you really care about your brother, you'll get him to a hospital!"

Bernie had come back out of the bathroom and stood listening to this exchange.

"Hey, when are we going to get some breakfast?"

Joe turned and glared at him and then back at Kim.

"Okay, fix us all some grub and make the coffee good and strong — I think we need some."

She went into the dingy kitchen and began making coffee, scrambled eggs (despite Bernie's request) and toast. The kitchen had improved some in appearance with her efforts, but its basic uncleanliness still sickened her. She dished up the food and took it back to Sheila and the men.

Sheila looked down as she reached out and took the plate. She had become much less vocal in the past twelve hours — no more complaints about not having McDonald's or Arby's. Kim thought it was a sign she was feeling ill — certainly that arm looked infected.

"You'd better eat some yourself," Joe said to her.

"Okay," Kim said, "but can I run downstairs and at least wash my face first?"

"Little miss sanitary Nursie," scoffed Bernie.

Joe looked at her.

"Okay, but be quick — we'll need some more coffee in a minute."

Kim tried not to run as she scurried across the room and down the basement stairs. Once inside her room, she shut the door quietly behind her and grabbed her two-meter rig from behind the stove.

"Pete," she whispered into the simplex frequency. "Are you still there?"

To her utter surprise, it was Marc's voice that came back to her.

"Kim! You okay?"

At the sound of his familiar voice, she burst into tears and found herself barely able to talk. Instantly, Pete's strong steady voice was talking to her.

"Kim! Listen! Stop crying, right now! What's happening?"

"They had me upstairs. Willy was conscious for just a few minutes. He really looks bad, and I think the woman, Sheila, is sick too. They had me make breakfast. I think they're going to try to make a break for it soon, and I think they'll kill me when they do." Her voice trailed off in sobs.

Now it was Marc talking to her.

"Kim, now don't cry, or Pete will take the mike back. Listen, we're right outside the cabin hidden behind some trees. How many guns do they have?"

"Joe and Bernie each have one, although Joe made Bernie give him his last night. I think Bernie would shoot him if he had the chance. Bernie wants to leave now, but Joe doesn't want to move his brother."

"Is there a lock on the front door?" Pete asked.

"A hook, I think," Kim said. "But they can see the front door from everywhere in the living room — they'd shoot me before I ever got it open.

"Oh no," Kim gasped. "I hear someone coming down the stairs!"

She dropped to her knees and shoved the rig behind the stove just as Joe opened the door. Desperately, she clasped her hands together and began praying aloud.

". . . and please give me the strength to get through this," she said fervently with her eyes closed.

There was silence from the doorway although she could feel Joe's eyes boring into her back. She kept her eyes closed and her head bowed.

"Okay, that's enough — I thought you just wanted to wash your face — didn't know you were going to conduct religious services," he said.

Kim got up, and avoiding his eyes, preceded him up the stairs. She could hear Willy making a strangling noise from the corner.

"I've got an idea," she said suddenly. "Let's boil some water and make a mist tent for him — might help his breathing."

Joe nodded his head okay. Kim went in the kitchen and filled the biggest pot she could find full of water. She turned the burner on high and set it to boil.

"We're going to need some sort of sheet," she told Joe.

The two of them looked around the cabin. A flimsy soiled gingham curtain hung over a window on the back wall. Joe ripped it down and handed it to her.

When the water was boiling hard, Kim carried the heavy kettle beside Willy's couch. She moved an empty crate up beside him and set the kettle on it. Next, she draped the curtain over the kettle and his head — holding it up several inches from his face with her hand. His breathing quickened as the steamy vapors penetrated his lungs. Kim felt the moisture from the steam running down her fingers underneath the cloth.

She tried to look confident as she sat holding the cloth, but she really had no idea whether this would help or not. A vague childhood memory of her mother using a vaporizer for her once when she had bronchitis was what had prompted the idea. Willy coughed and stirred slightly.

* * * * * * * * * * * * * * * * * *

Outside in the underbrush, Marc and Pete lay, desperately listening for Kim.

"What do we do now?" Marc whispered to Pete.

"Call for help," Pete answered.

Chapter 17

Making Plans

Bankrobber's Cabin
Noon

Kim wracked her brain frantically, trying to think of another excuse to get back downstairs even for a moment. The steady struggle of Willy's labored breathing filled the small room, and for a while even Sheila seemed to be watching the young man's fight to breathe. The focus of the room was Willy's respiration. Kim knew it was useless to ask to go to the basement. She kept busy, boiling new pots of water to keep the kettle under the makeshift tent covering Willy full of steam.

She could hear the fluid rattling in his chest as he coughed every once in a while, After an hour or so, it seemed to her that his breathing was becoming a little easier. She pulled the sheet back and wiped the moisture from his face. He opened his eyes and stared at her.

"Willy?" she said softly.

"Yes," he croaked.

"Here," she said, lifting his head up a little. "Try to drink some water."

She gently poured a little water into his dry mouth — most of it ran out the sides, but he valiantly tried to swallow and some of it went down his throat. Kim kept coaxing him until he had consumed almost an ounce of liquid.

"Thank you," he whispered.

Kim looked over at Joe to see if he was taking in this scene. She was surprised when she saw Joe avert his eyes and look at the floor.

Why, he doesn't want to admit what kind of condition his brother is in! Kim thought. *He's trying to shut him out.*

Bernie stood up and walked over in front of Joe. In a low, restrained voice, he asked a question.

"Okay, Boss, what are we going to do?"

Joe turned his back so that he couldn't see Willy.

"We're going to leave — tonight just after dark. I've got a friend in Sacramento — if we can get that far, he may be able to get some help for Willy."

"Why don't you just leave him here?" Bernie asked. "You could call the police from a couple of hundred miles down the road and tell them where he is."

Kim felt her hopes soar at this possibility.

"I would stay and take care of him," she interjected into the conversation.

Joe ignored her comment completely.

"Willy goes where I go, and that's final!"

"I think you're going to be hauling a dead body, man — just look at him," Bernie said in disgust as he lit a cigarette and began pacing, all the while scratching at his backside frantically.

Sheila laughed maliciously. "Has your poison oak spread a little, Bernie?"

"Shut up!" Bernie shouted.

"Shut up yourself, and I thought I told you not to smoke in here," Joe yelled back at him.

Bernie slammed the door behind him as he stomped outside. Sheila began whimpering.

"My arm hurts so bad," she moaned. "And I feel hot and cold all over."

Joe looked over at her but then buried his head in his hands, deep in thought. When Bernie came back in, the odor of cigarette smoke surrounding him, Joe motioned for him to sit on the floor near him.

"Look," Joe told him. "We're going to need another car for tonight. By now, they've surely got a stolen report out on this one."

"Okay," Bernie said. "Give me the distributor cap back, and I'll drive into town and see what I can locate. I need some more beer and cigarettes, anyway."

Joe narrowed his eyes as he stared at Bernie.

"You'd like that — wouldn't you? Just you and the van."

"Oh sure," snickered Bernie. "Like where would I go? — you've got the money — you've got both guns."

"And you're not going to have the van," retorted Joe.

"So how am I supposed to find another one? — walk into town — or do you have a horse hidden somewhere?" Bernie asked sarcastically.

"You don't have to walk into town — just take a hike up and down the road here and check out the local cabins. There's got to be somebody around — then tonight, after dark, we make our move."

"If you like exercise so much, why don't you take the walk?" Bernie grumbled.

Joe just pointed toward the door and then rested his hand on the two guns, now sitting beside him on the table. Bernie cursed and slammed out the door.

Once he was gone, the tension in the cabin relaxed visibly. Joe moved over to Sheila and gently examined her arm.

"Come here," he beckoned to Kim.

For once, Sheila didn't protest when Kim got close to her. Kim kept her hands behind her — she regarded Sheila with the same caution she would a caged lioness, but she bent forward and looked at the swollen arm that Joe probed cautiously with his fingers.

"What do you think?" Joe asked.

Kim shrugged.

"She needs antibiotics — just like Willy," she said simply. "She could have blood poisoning, and that could kill her if you don't do something."

Sheila's eyes widened in alarm.

"Just relax," Joe told her, patting her hand. "By this time tomorrow, you and Willy will both have antibiotics. What can we do in the meantime?" he asked Kim.

"I suppose you could try soaking her arm in hot water — might make it feel better," Kim said.

Sheila made little sniffling sounds and pulled her arm back from Joe.

"You promised to take care of me — you're just as no good as Bernie," she said to Joe.

"Go put some more water on to boil," Joe directed Kim, and then to Sheila, he added, "I don't remember any promises — watch your tongue, woman!"

Sheila turned her head away and kept on crying noisily as Joe got up and went to stand in front of the small window near the woodstove.

Kim hoped fervently that Marc and Pete were out of sight. Suddenly, she had a new fear: if they tried to do something like rush the cabin, they might be shot too! Her hands shook as she filled the tea kettle full of water and put it on the stove. She knew she had to warn them not to try entering the cabin.

Willy was asleep. His soft snoring rumbled through the room. *He must be feeling better,* Kim thought. *First time, I've heard him really sleeping in two days.*

When the water began to boil, Kim poured some in a dented aluminum basin and carried it to Sheila. She laid two ragged cloths in Sheila's lap.

"It's awkward with the wound that high up your arm, but maybe you can soak the rags and wrap them around. I'll help you if you want," Kim told her.

Sheila ignored her and picked up one of the cloths and dropped it in the water.

"Ouch!" she said, pulling back her fingers. "You trying to burn me or what?"

"It's plenty cold in this cabin," Kim said. "That water will be cool before you know it."

Gingerly, Sheila swished the rag in the water and then tried to wring it out with her good hand. When she lifted the rag to her arm, water dripped all over her. Angrily, she looked at Kim.

"Wring it out for me," she commanded.

Kim grabbed the rag between her hands and squeezed the excess water out. She handed it to Sheila who laid it carefully on her sore arm. She let out a slight gasp as the heat touched the inflamed skin but then settled back in the chair with a more eased expression on her face.

144

With Willy asleep and Sheila pacified, Kim turned to Joe. Rubbing her hand across her forehead, she said, "Could I just go lie down for an hour? — my head really hurts."

"Lie down over there on the sleeping bag by the stove," Joe commanded. "I don't want to have to go down the stairs every time we need you."

"But I can't sleep up here with everyone talking," Kim protested.

"Oh, we'll all be quiet for Miss Nursie so she can have her nap time," Sheila laughed nastily. "Pretty soon, she's going to get a nice long nap."

"Shut up, Sheila!" Joe barked. He pointed at the sleeping bag, and reluctantly, Kim went over to it and lay down. It smelled sour, just like the whole cabin. She turned her back to Joe and Willy and stared at the flickering fire through the slots of the woodstove. She really was tired and she laid her head against her arm and closed her eyes. *How on earth can I think of sleeping when they're talking about killing me?* she wondered. But her whole body was so exhausted that for a couple of minutes she actually dozed.

It was only silent until Bernie came back in the cabin, slamming the door behind him with such a bang that Willy let out a groan. Kim kept her eyes shut and pretended to be asleep.

"Well, did you find one?" Joe asked.

"Yeah, there's a Suburban van down the road — I could see the people out fishing behind their cabin. Looks like they're here to stay awhile. They've got laundry strung out between a couple of trees."

"A Suburban's got windows all around, doesn't it?" Joe asked.

"Yeah, but they've got the rear ones painted with that metallic stuff — you can't see in," Bernie answered.

"Okay, let's wait until midnight — make sure they're asleep, and then take it," Joe said.

"Won't be hard either," Bernie said. "I looked in the window, and they've left the keys in — only problem is if the engine starting wakes them up."

"Is that the only car there?" Joe asked.

"Looks like it."

"Well, then they won't have any way to follow, and I doubt that cabin has a phone — don't know of one along here that does," Joe said. "Someone will have to walk into town to report it unless they've got a CB or something."

"If we're going to bug out, why don't we hit a bank or store on the way?" Bernie suggested. "We could sure use some more money."

Joe shook his head.

"Don't you realize how critical it'll be to get out of here? There'll be plenty of time for jobs in California after we get everyone well," Joe said.

"What about? . . ." Bernie left a significant pause, and although Kim's back was turned, she felt certain he was pointing at her.

There was silence in the cabin. She knew they were making gestures at each other. When Bernie chuckled softly, Kim felt her skin crawl.

I've got to do something! she thought desperately. Almost as if helping her, Willy coughed and groaned. Kim rolled over and looked across the room at his restless figure under the steam tent.

"See what you can do," Joe said.

She got up and went over to Willy. The cloth over him was soaked wet. It didn't really matter — any new cloth would get wet quickly, too, but maybe she could use it as an excuse to run downstairs.

"There's a curtain hanging over the closet in the basement. Let me go get it and change it for this one — it's wringing wet," she said to Joe.

"Okay," he said waving her toward the door.

As she got up, Bernie stood up too. Her heart sank as his heavy footsteps followed her across the room. She ran down the stairs quickly and breathed a sigh of relief when she heard him stop at the head of the stairs. Hurriedly, she snatched the two- meter rig and stuffed it in the pocket of the over-sized pants she was wearing. Then she grabbed the curtain and

146

gave it a hard yank. The aging, faded material ripped away easily, and she threw the cloth over her arm and ran back upstairs. She took the cloth to the kitchen and shook the dust into the sink before carrying it back to spread over Willy. It wasn't any dirtier than the one she had been using before, but she didn't envy him having to inhale the damp musty odor.

Once she had him settled with a fresh pot of boiling water, she returned to the sleeping bag by the fire. She tucked herself inside it, revolted by its smell but needing cover for what she was about to try. She turned on her right side so that her back was to the men. Sheila's chair was practically next to her head, but the woman appeared to be napping.

Slowly, Kim pulled her transceiver from her left pocket with her left hand. For once, she was grateful to be left-handed as she was going to have to operate the rig without benefit of her right arm which was under her. She moved the rig next to her stomach and turned the volume control all the way down with her left hand before turning it on. There was no static rush noise to tell her it was on, but she would just have to assume it was.

As she had done in the van the night she was kidnapped, Kim began sending Morse code on the key pad.

"MARC IF POLICE THERE, DO NOT COME UNLESS I SEND I FOR IN"

Kim continued sending instructions. How she wished she could turn up the volume and see if Marc heard her, but she knew she was taking a great risk just in doing what she was. She decided on the letter "O" for coming out. "If I'm going to try to escape, I'll send 'O' first," she sent. " 'I' for in; 'O' for out." She sent the same message three times, then turned the rig off and stuffed it back in her pocket.

Joe and Bernie were talking quietly, making plans in earnest.

"When you bring the van back, you and I can carry Willy on the cushions and lay him in the back. Sheila can ride in the front with you, and I'll stay in the back with Willy. We'll follow 34 east so we don't have to go back past the cabin — it will take an hour to connect up with the freeway again, but then we'll be on our way. By the time those people can do anything about their car being gone, we should be in Roseburg."

There was no mention made of Kim except for a laugh from Bernie. Kim she assumed they might be gesturing at her again. And then silence. She shuddered and closed her eyes tight.

Chapter 18

We Have Found the Girl!

Outside the Cabin
December 27th — 1:30 p.m.

"We have found the girl!" That was the message Pete Sheffield had just relayed to the sheriff's office through another ham on the Newport repeater. Pete and Marc lay motionless on the cold, wet ground — both of them with their handhelds to their ears. Marc was monitoring the simplex frequency while Pete talked to a deputy via a phone patch.

"What is your location?" the sheriff's deputy asked.

"We're up Highway 34, but I think it's too dangerous to bring marked cars in here right now. One of us will meet you somewhere and direct you," Pete told him.

"We advise that you both leave the scene immediately and meet us at the junction of 101 and 34," was the reply from the sheriff's office.

"Understood," Pete said quietly into the microphone.

He motioned to Marc to slide backward until they were no longer visible over the crest of the hill. They had a hurried conference.

"You go; I'll stay," Marc said emphatically.

Pete looked at the young man. He thought of all the ways this scene could end. Images of gunfire and Marc rushing the door flashed through his mind. He saw Marc lying on the ground, mortally wounded as he had seen many young men in Vietnam.

"No," he told Marc firmly. "I outrank you on this one."

Marc raised his eyebrows quizzically.

"Retired Air Force Colonel," Pete said.

"That only counts if I'm in the military, too," Marc replied with determination.

"Look, Marc. I know you want to do the best for your girlfriend. And now that you've gotten me mixed up in this, I do too. The sheriff wants us both to meet him. I can understand why, but I do think one of us should stay right here and monitor simplex while the other one goes to get help from the law. And, I think that someone who stays should be me. Now, don't argue!"

Marc stared at Pete for a full minute before he mumbled "Okay."

"But, I'll stay on simplex, too, so in case anything happens, I can come right back," he said.

"Agreed," Pete, said, clapping Marc on the shoulder. "Now start the car as quietly as you can and go a little ways down the road before you turn around in case anyone's listening."

Marc crawled back fifty feet or so before he stood up and ran to the car. He did as Pete instructed, and soon he was traveling as fast as he dared back down Highway 34 to Waldport. Two sheriff's patrol cars were waiting for him on the corner.

Sgt. Neil Fisher greeted him as he got out of the car.

Despite his determination to remain calm, Marc found the words tumbling out as he portrayed the drama going on in the cabin.

"And she's sending Morse code to us — says she'll let us know if she wants us to come in or if she's going to try to make a break for it. That's why Pete stayed behind — to listen for her signal."

Sgt. Fisher's face looked alarmed at this news. He turned to one of the other officers.

"I want a SWAT team and a Safety team immediately. We'll need to set up a base somewhere — get them organized, and I'll radio the rendezvous point in a few minutes."

"Let me talk to your friend," Sgt. Fisher said to Marc.

"KH6XM from KA7ITR. How's it going, Pete?" Marc said into his two-meter microphone.

"KA7ITR from KH6XM — all's quiet, Marc. No movement I can see at all. Have you found the sheriff's people?"

Sgt. Fisher took the microphone from him.

"This is Sgt. Fisher from Lincoln County Sheriff's Department speaking. Sir, we would like you to leave the area while we get our people in place."

"I understand your concern, Sergeant. First, let me tell you that I'm 63 years old — a retired Air Force Colonel and a retired commercial airlines pilot. I didn't get to be this old by doing anything stupid, so don't worry on my account. I'm not visible at all to anyone in the cabin, but I think you need to have someone watching until you can get all set up."

Sgt. Fisher nodded. Pete's calm voice reassured him that he was dealing with someone who wouldn't take rash action.

"Okay, Colonel. Just stand by. We're getting help organized as fast as we can — I'll be there in just a few minutes to check out the situation."

He motioned for Marc and two officers to get in the car with him. They drove back up the Alsea Highway until they were about one hundred yards from the rutted dirt road that led to the cabin.

"There," said Marc pointing. "The cabin's right over that hill. Drive on past it — that's what we did."

They parked the car around the bend just as Marc had done. Before the sergeant could protest, Marc was out of the car and leading the way through the thick underbrush. The four of them came across Pete just below the crest of the hill. He motioned for them to crouch down beside him. Flattened out on the cold, damp ground, they had a hurried conference.

"Do you know what part of the house she's in?" Sgt. Fisher asked.

"Probably upstairs, now," Pete said. "They only let her go to the basement when she's not taking care of the guy who's wounded. I gather they aren't letting her go to the basement at all now — that's probably why she's sending code."

"How's she managing that?" the sergeant asked.

"Like this," Marc demonstrated, pushing one of the numbers on his touchtone pad in rhythmic fashion. A clear beeping noise came out of the transceiver. "Or she could be holding down one of the touchtone keys and sending the code with her thumb on the push to talk button."

"Supposing they see her?" the sergeant queried.

"Her rig's really small," Marc said. "I bet she has it in her pocket — that's where she carried it in the hospital. And I'm sure she's got the volume all the way down so they don't hear her."

"Okay, listen," Sgt. Fisher said to Pete. "You continue to monitor for us here while Marc and I set up a base down the road somewhere. If you see the slightest movement, call me immediately. Officers Wilby and Terhes will stay here with you until we get the SWAT team in place.

"I don't want anyone to try anything," he said emphatically, "unless it's absolutely necessary — understood?"

Pete and the two officers nodded in agreement and Sgt. Fisher and Marc crawled down the embankment for a few yards and then stood up and ran to the patrol car.

Sgt. Fisher put the car in reverse and turned around and started heading back down the road. About a quarter of a mile down the road, he stopped at a small frame house painted blue, hidden among the trees. A new silver Honda was parked out front.

"Stay here," Sgt. Fisher told Marc.

He got out of the car and went up to the front door. Marc watched as he talked with a white-haired man and his wife in the doorway. Apparently, they invited him in as the sergeant disappeared from view. A few minutes later, he came back out on the porch, shook hands with the elderly couple, and sprinted back to the car.

"That's going to be our base," he said to Marc. "Couple on a fishing vacation — rented the cabin from someone in town."

Sgt. Fisher grabbed his microphone as he started the squad car back down the driveway.

"We'll need a couple of plain cars," he told the dispatcher at the sheriff's office. "The teams can come in a van — looked like there was plenty of room to park it out of sight behind the house."

He drove rapidly back down to where the other men were waiting.

"Let's see if we can get hold of a utility company truck to put some plain clothesmen in," Sgt. Fisher told one officer. He drew a quick sketch for the other officers of how to locate the cabin they would be using for a base of operations.

"Marc?" came Pete's quiet voice over the two-meter rig.

"I'm here — what's happening?" Marc replied.

"The cabin door just opened, and there's a guy — probably mid-thirties with dark hair standing there smoking a cigarette."

Sgt. Fisher took the microphone from Marc.

"Can you see anyone else?" he asked.

"No, just this one guy — looks about six feet, — maybe 180 pounds — has on a plaid shirt and jeans.

"Now, he's closed the door behind him. He's just standing there, smoking and scratching."

"Scratching?" the sergeant asked.

"Yeah, scratching his backside really hard — must itch really bad. If he wanders this way — oops forget that thought — he just went back inside."

Sgt. Fisher didn't even ask Pete what his idea was — he knew what he'd do under the circumstances — probably try to tackle the guy. He turned to two officers standing by a patrol car.

"Marc, stay here. Lt. Keller is on his way here from Lincoln City — he'll want to run the operations base — we'll put you in charge of communications. In the meantime, I want to go back to the office to see if I can expedite the teams. When the lieutenant arrives, show him where the cabin is we want to use for a base. I'll have the necessary radio gear sent up to you so we can all be in touch."

After Sgt. Fisher left, Marc stood alone with the one remaining sheriff's deputy.

"You ever been in a situation like this before?" Marc asked him.

"No," the other man sort of half-laughed. "On the coast here, the most exciting thing we usually run into is unemployed fishermen and loggers getting in bar room brawls. Don't worry, though," he said, noting Marc's drawn face.

"Lt. Keller and Sgt. Fisher both have worked in Portland before coming here. They definitely know what they're doing."

"I hope so," Marc muttered. "I just feel so frustrated, standing here like a third thumb."

Marc didn't have long to feel useless, as soon Lt. Keller came driving up with three other officers. Introductions were made quickly, and soon Marc was in the car with them driving up to the retired couple's cabin they were going to use as a base station.

To Marc's surprise, the couple had packed a bag and were getting ready to leave.

"We figured we'd just be in the way so we're going to go down to Coos Bay and visit our daughter for a day or so," the man told Lt. Keller.

"Well, that's very understanding of you, sir," the lieutenant said. "Give me the phone number where you'll be, and we'll give you a call as soon as this situation is under control."

Marc carried their suitcase for them to the car. The woman looked at him with sympathy.

"From the look on your face, son, I bet this girl hostage is a friend of yours," she said.

"Yes, she is — a very special friend," Marc said quietly.

"Well, you try not to worry too much — I'm sure the officers are doing everything they can," the woman said, patting him on the back.

"Come on, Martha — let's get on the road," her husband said.

The two of them got in the car. Marc waved goodbye quickly and ran back into the house. Just then, a small sheriff's van pulled up and two officers got out carrying radios for the base station. Marc watched as they quickly set up the gear on the dining room table. Within minutes, they were on

154

the air and Lt. Keller was in contact with both the Newport and Lincoln County offices. He motioned for Marc to sit down beside him.

"We'd like you to write down your messages from Pete and put down the time of each," he told Marc. "Any news from him?"

"Just a second, I'll check," Marc said. "KH6XM from KA7ITR, — how's it going, Pete?"

"Just a wisp of smoke coming out of the chimney," Pete replied. "Otherwise, everything is quiet."

"Roger, Pete. I'm going off frequency just a minute to talk to Jim monitoring the Newport repeater. I want to tell him to call us on simplex if by any chance Kim should switch back to the repeater. I doubt she will though — sounded to me, like she was lucky to be doing what she was."

Just then, the SWAT team arrived along with Sgt. Fisher. They poured into the living room and began outlining plans for surrounding the cabin.

"I'd sure like to know the floorplan of that place," one man said.

The officer who had taken over communications beside Marc nodded.

"Let me call the assessor's office and see what we can find out," he said.

Marc listened to the hurried conversations in the room. Three men dressed as power-company employees had arrived in a utility truck. Apparently, they were also going to be stationed in the area. Something called a "Safety Team" was going to be responsible for Kim's safety if they could get to her.

If they could get to her! Marc looked around the room at all the various rifles and handguns the men were carrying and shuddered.

Chapter 19

A Long Afternoon

In the Cabin
3 p.m.

"**C**abin fever — that's what we've got," Bernie snorted, looking at Willy, fighting for every breath and at Sheila whose face was becoming more flushed with each hour. "Can't you see what's happening?" he yelled angrily at Joe. "They're sick — both of them, really sick. And you're going to sit here and die right with them! What time is it anyway?"

Joe shrugged his shoulders and pointed at Kim who had the only working watch among them. She lay motionless, apparently napping in the sleeping bag by the woodstove. Bernie went over and nudged her with his foot. Her eyes flew open in alarm.

"Hey Nursie — what time is it?"

Kim pulled her arm out from the sleeping bag and looked at her watch.

"Almost three," she said softly.

"Three o'clock and you want to wait until ten you said," Bernie growled, again turning to Joe. "Well, I ain't waiting until no ten o'clock. It's dark by four thirty — at five you make your decision. Either I go and get the van then or I'm walking out. I'll be better on my own than stuck with a bunch of dead meat."

Joe scowled at him, trying to guess whether he was bluffing or not. He needed Bernie — there was no way he could make it across the border with two sick people without someone to help him. And Bernie needed him — needed the money, needed Joe's contacts, but he sensed that Bernie was telling the truth when he said he was about ready to leave.

If Bernie did desert them, probably the first thing he'd do would be to hold up a store. If he were caught, it would just be a matter of time before the police found the cabin.

"So how about it, huh?" Bernie asked. "When I leave at five, is it to get a car or just to leave?"

"If you'll wait until seven it's to get a car — we've got to at least wait until the commuter traffic is gone before we hit I-5," Joe said. "But," he added, eyeing the two guns on the table beside him, "you'll do it without a gun."

"What?" Bernie shouted, shocking Willy into consciousness and eliciting a weak groan from him. "What?" he yelled again. "Without a gun? Supposing someone takes a shot at me — what am I supposed to do — just stand there and flap my wings?"

"I guess you'll have to make sure no one sees you," Joe said evenly. "If I keep your gun, there's a better chance you'll come back for us."

Bernie cursed, grabbed his pack of cigarettes, and slammed out the front door. A moment later, there was the sound of a rotted board breaking and the weight of Bernie's body crashing through the porch.

Kim looked at Joe, her eyes wide with fear. To her surprise, Joe was laughing.

"My cousin always said that porch needed fixing — been saying that for the last twenty years. We knew where all the bad boards were — guess Bernie doesn't though," Joe said.

Almost instantly, Bernie came stomping back through the door. Kim cringed at the stream of swear words he let loose as he limped into the room and reached down to roll up his torn pant leg. Blood dripped from a ragged gash on his calf.

"Looks like I'm the only healthy one left," Joe said sarcastically, tossing Bernie a rag to staunch the flow of blood.

"You! Nursie!" Bernie commanded Kim. "Do something!"

Quietly, Kim got out of the sleeping bag and reached for the hydrogen peroxide left on the floor near Sheila. She went into the kitchen and grabbed the last fairly clean dish towel from the counter. Cautiously, she knelt by Bernie's leg. He howled when she applied the peroxide to the cut which was already stopping bleeding on its own. She doubted that the peroxide hurt at all, but she certainly wasn't going to suggest that to Bernie. As quickly as she could, she tore the towel into strips and wrapped it in a bandage around the man's leg. The blood stained through but then stopped.

"Now how am I am going to walk with this?" he demanded of Joe.

"You'll walk," Joe said quietly, fingering the gun on the table beside him.

Bernie muttered something unintelligible and limped off to the bathroom. Kim gathered up the scanty first aid supplies and put them on the kitchen counter. She wet a cloth and went back over to tend Willy. If her makeshift oxygen tent had helped at first, it wasn't now. She could hear the deep gurgling of fluid in his chest. He didn't respond as she bathed his face with fresh water. It would only be a matter of hours until he died, she feared.

And what about my own life? she thought miserably. She closed her eyes, trying to imagine what was going on outside. If the police rushed the cabin, she felt there was a very good chance she would get shot in the exchange of fire. She scanned the cabin, trying to decide where she would seek cover if gunfire started. *Maybe, behind the woodstove,* she thought. *But knowing these men, one of them would probably grab her as a shield. Should she try to make a run for it now? No.* She knew she would be shot before she ever reached the door.

"How's he doing?" Joe asked gruffly, interrupting her thoughts.

"Not good," Kim replied honestly. "I don't think he's conscious."

"Hey Willy!" Joe yelled.

Willy moaned and stirred slightly. Apparently, he was still conscious of his surroundings or of sound at least. Kim adjusted the pillows behind him and folded the steam tent.

"Why are you taking that away?" Joe asked suspiciously. "I thought you said it was helping him."

"I think it did for awhile, but he seems so hot, I thought we'd just let him be out in the air for awhile and see how he does."

Joe looked as if he didn't believe her, but he didn't protest. He began pacing in the small room and talking aloud.

"Okay, Bernie gets back with the car by eight — we're loaded and out of here in a couple of minutes. That should put us in Corvallis by nine, on I - 5 by nine thirty — maybe to the border by one. We'll stop in Yreka and get some help for Willy and Sheila — should be smooth sailing from then on."

He spoke in a convincing tone, but Kim noticed the expression on his face looked anything but believing. With the deep circles under his eyes and his unshaven face, Joe looked as if he had aged ten years in the last two days.

I probably don't look so great myself, Kim thought, running her fingers through her hair. "I'll make some coffee," she said quietly and edged back into the kitchen.

She put the kettle on to boil and then reached into her pocket.

"Bernie leaving 7 p.m. to steal car — no gun," she sent in code.

"Hey, Nursie! — what's taking you so long?" Bernie yelled.

Kim hurried to the doorway.

"The water's just starting to boil — I'll have the coffee ready in just a second."

Her hands shook as she poured some coffee in the awkward drip apparatus she had fashioned with some paper towels and an old jar. She took a deep breath as the boiling water seeped through the grounds and dripped into the clear jar.

As long as I can keep them drinking coffee and doing things that civilized people do, maybe it will keep their minds off killing me, she thought fervently. That thought was short-lived though. Bernie took one sip of the coffee and threw his cup on the floor, splashing the hot liquid all over Kim's legs.

"Stuff tastes like rat poison," he declared angrily. "What are you trying to do? Poison us?"

160

Kim shook her head "no" vigorously and retreated to the kitchen to get a rag.

"Shut up, Bernie," Joe said. "The stuff's okay — beats prison coffee anyway."

Just then, Sheila woke up with a whimper.

"Are we going to go to California pretty soon?" she whined. "My arm's killing me."

"Pretty soon, Baby — pretty soon," Joe soothed her.

Kim mopped up the spilled coffee with some paper towels and picked up Bernie's cup without comment. Her leg stung where the boiling liquid had seeped through the pant leg. As she turned to go back to the kitchen, she heard Joe talking to Sheila.

"Bernie's getting us a van and we'll be leaving around eight," he told her.

"What about *her*?" Sheila said. Kim could feel Sheila's eyes boring into her back.

"Bernie and I will take care of everything, Baby. You just close your eyes and go back to sleep."

Kim grabbed the kitchen sink for support. She looked at her watch. Four o'clock. She had less than four hours to live unless ... unless what? Unless someone from the outside could save her or she could save herself. She glanced frantically at the one small kitchen window.

* * * * * * * * * * * * * * * * * *

Outside the Cabin
4 p.m.

Sgt. Fisher wriggled up the cold muddy embankment to join Pete Sheffield just below the crest of the hill.

"She just signaled," Pete told him. "Said one of the guys is coming out unarmed at seven o'clock to steal a car. I just relayed that information to Marc at the base cabin you set up."

"Unarmed? Wonder how's she sure of that? We'll certainly treat him as though he is armed," Sgt. Fisher said.

"What are you going to do?" Pete asked.

"Well nothing right here where it would make any commotion. We've got plainclothesmen in place up and down the road all ready. Traffic has been stopped in both directions. An FBI. Swat team is on the way from Portland and a Safety team is coming from Salem. Just got a call from Lieutenant Keller — the men are assembled and on their way — once they get here, they'll have a planning session in Newport and then they'll be here."

Sgt. Fisher pulled his hand-held radio from his belt and held it close to his mouth.

"Position A from Fisher — any movement out back?"

"Negative," was the man's reply.

"Position A — come back down out of sight."

"Roger."

"Where's he?" Pete whispered.

"Up a utility pole about 25 yards south of the back of the cabin — he's dressed as a line repairman."

"XM from ITR"

"Go ahead, Marc," Pete said.

"One of the officers has gone to the assessor's office to see if he can find a floorplan for the cabin. He's not back yet, but another officer just brought us a drawing. Seems one of the hams in Waldport monitoring this whole scene is familiar with the cabin we've been describing. Knows the owner and has been inside several times. He drew out a floorplan and brought it up to the roadblock. Someone will be delivering it up to you guys in just a minute."

Sgt. Fisher nodded at the information, and Pete said "Roger" into the microphone. There was a rustling in the bushes behind them, and Pete and the sergeant turned to see an officer hurrying through the underbrush with a paper in his hand.

"No time to photocopy this now," the officer said breathlessly, "but Lt. Keller wants you guys to see this before I take it back down to the SWAT team."

Sgt. Fisher and Pete pored over the drawing. The cabin looked simple enough — just one living area with a small bathroom and kitchen in alcoves off to the side. There were stairs sketched in leading to the basement. The front door was drawn in. Sgt. Fisher pulled out a pen and carefully drew in the porch including the broken boards they had witnessed Bernie break through a short while ago. He added every tree and shrub that could be used as cover for the men.

"SWAT guys will want this," Fisher said. "Looks like we could get through that front window if we had to, but it'd be tight," added the sergeant, sketching in the window and marking it and the door with x's.

"Show this to the two guys over there, and then take it on back," Sgt. Fisher said, motioning to two other sheriff's officers positioned farther down the ridge.

"Are you going to rush the cabin?" Pete asked.

"Not unless we have to — it will depend a lot on what happens at seven o'clock when this guy is supposedly coming out."

Pete thought again of the young woman trapped inside the cabin with these desperate men. An expert in Morse code, he had detected some nervousness in her sending, but it was still remarkably steady and even, considering the circumstances.

Come on Kim — hang in there! he voiced silently in his brain.

* * * * * * * * * * * * * * * * * *

Base Cabin
4:15 p.m.

Someone had built a fire in the small woodstove near him, and Marc felt the welcome warmth at his back. Although he longed to be with Pete up near the cabin where Kim was being held, he fully realized the importance of his position here. He had copied Kim's message at the same time that Pete did, but it was good to have someone to double check with. Lt. Keller was standing nearby, in case Marc got any more information from Kim.

The same Amateur Radio operator who had brought the cabin drawing to the roadblock had also brought three more two- meter rigs so that Marc could monitor the repeater frequencies too.

Quickly, the ham community established a net control on each frequency so that Marc need only listen to information passed on by the net control person. The offers to help had been instantaneous. Marc relayed Lt. Keller's suggestion that a few of them report to the roadblock just east of Waldport to bring coffee and food and assist the officers on duty. He looked at his watch. 4:30 p.m. Two and a half hours until the man named Bernie would be coming out of the cabin. Marc wished that he could be the one to get his hands on that guy directly. He felt the muscles in his body tense at the idea but then relax as he turned his attention back to Pete, who was checking in.

Chapter 20

Hostage — Code Five!

Newport Sheriff's Office
5 p.m.

L ieutenant Keller pushed chairs out of the way to make room for the ten men, all of them dressed in off-black military fatigues, pouring into the room. The five members of the FBI SWAT (Special Weapons and Tactics) team had arrived almost simultaneously with the five-member Safety team from Salem. The Safety team's job would be to back up the SWAT team and to get the hostage to safety if possible.

The attire of the men did nothing to brighten the dark winter night nor the mood surrounding this assignment.

"It's not going to be easy," said Lt. Keller, drawing a sketch of the cabin on the blackboard. "If we rush the cabin, we may lose the girl — but if we wait too long, they may kill her."

He explained the rest of the details of the situation to the Special Agent in Charge of the SWAT team and then backed away so that the Special Agent could take charge. Although the men knew each other's names, they referred to each other by their tactical titles — "Agent One, Agent Two, etc."

"How big are those trees by Corner #2?" asked Agent Four.

Lt. Keller stood up and pointed to the drawing of the cabin with its four numbered corners.

"They'll easily conceal one, maybe two men — ditto for the shrubs on Corner 1. The only cover by Corner 3 is the van, but from what I saw of the area, I would guess Corners 1 and 3 would be your best bet.

The Special Agent in Charge wrinkled his forehead as he studied the drawing.

"How high off the ground is the porch?" he asked.

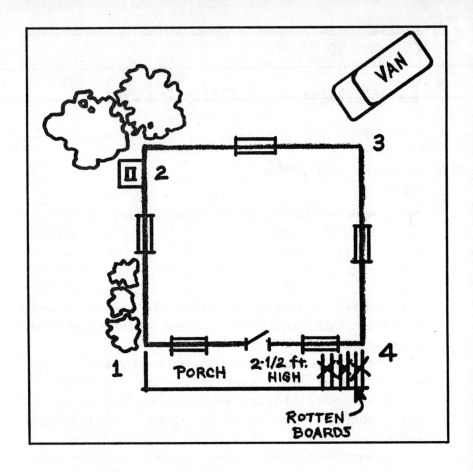

"About two and a half feet — and the boards about three feet to the left of Corner 4 are rotted. Our men saw one of the suspects break through when he came outside for a minute." Lt. Keller said.

The Special Agent in Charge made marks indicating the bad boards in the porch.

"I think we can hide two Safety people right here under the porch," he said as men in the room nodded in agreement.

"And another one here," he said indicating the back of the stolen van, "and a fourth one here," he said pointing to a bush near Corner 1.

Lt. Keller stood silently as the men conferred. He knew that the **Final Decision** whether to accept the assignment as it had been presented lay with them. If the Special Agent in Charge felt that the plan was unduly hazardous, he could ask for changes or refuse it altogether, though Lt. Keller could not think of any assignments they had ever refused. With their M-16s slung over their shoulders and their holstered .357 revolvers, the black-clad men wearing both light and heavy bulletproof armor looked like they could invade anything.

"Okay, let's go," the Special Agent in Charge said. The men pulled black wool stocking caps on over their visored ball caps to protect them from both the rain and the cold.

"I'll have a fire and medic backup follow you in," Lt. Keller said.

The Special Agent in Charge nodded as they quietly loaded in the waiting van outside the door. The men sat down on the metal benches inside the van. All conversation quieted as the driver started the engine and started down the coast highway toward Waldport — just ten men in black in a black van racing through a black night to rescue a hostage.

* * * * * * * * * * * * * * * * * * *

The call "Code Five" had gone out hours ago, meaning to secure the area and to follow all the precautions used in a hostage situation. As the black van approached the roadblock, Officer Kent Marklee stood back to let them through. He happened to know the driver — Special Agent #1 was Mike Fetherton — his cousin, but under the directions of "Code Five" no show of recognition was made by either of them.

The van turned up the Alsea Highway and made its way along the deserted winding road. A couple of the men shifted uneasily on the bench, and the scratching noise of the velcro fasteners on their safety holsters broke the silence. One man reached down and fastened his a little tighter. Each man had his own reasons for being willing to risk his life for a total stranger, but it was a subject they rarely discussed.

They drove beyond the cabin and parked behind the clump of trees where Marc and Pete had parked earlier in the day. Quietly, the men left the back door and immediately became part of the darkness, creeping silently to their preassigned positions.

Pete and Sgt. Fisher turned in surprise as the Special Agent in Charge crept up behind them. He motioned for the two of them to back down off the rise overlooking the cabin.

Pete stared at the man dressed all in black. Except for the letters FBI on the back of his bulletproof vest, he could have been a military commando. *I can see why they're known for their infantry-like tactics — I didn't even hear him come up on us,* Pete thought. At a glance, he took in the grenades hanging from the man's belt. *Just like Vietnam, he thought, except that I bet these are flash-bang grenades without shrapnel. They're used to "divert and disorient" the suspects.*

"You need to stay close enough to hear her signal," the agent whispered to him in the darkness, "but we want you completely out of any possible line of fire."

He motioned for Pete and Sgt. Fisher to follow him through the underbrush to a hidden place behind some logs. The Special Agent in Charge tapped his radio mike clipped to his shoulder and said to Sgt. Fisher, "If she says she's coming out or wants us to come in, we have to know immediately — understand?"

Sgt. Fisher nodded.

"Her life may depend on how fast you tell the sergeant here and how fast he tells us — do you understand?" he asked again, turning to Pete.

Pete nodded. He did understand. And that understanding made his heart pound against his ribs in the cold darkness.

* * * * * * * * * * * * * * * * * * *

A fox couldn't have been more quiet. Agents One and Two hid behind the shrubs on Corner 1. While Agent One covered him, Agent Two moved stealthily across the short open space to the corner of the house. From his vantage point, he could cover two sides of the house. He knew that Agent Four was diagonally across from him on Corner 3, covering the other two sides. There was a slight glow of light coming from the front window — more like from a woodstove than from a lamp. He could smell the pungent odor of burning Douglas fir wood in the damp air. If only he could get close enough to the window to peek in, but that wasn't in the plan — they were to do nothing that might endanger Kim.

* * * * * * * * * * * * * * * * * * *

Special Agent Four crouched beside the stolen van. Slowly he inched his way forward until he was even with the left rear fender. He was less than a foot from the corner of the house. The moonless night increased the blackness so he had to rely on his keen eyes to pick up anything at all. Something was a little different on the wall joining Corners Three and Four of the house. He leaned forward and peered down the rough-hewn wood surface. A window. There was a small window — maybe no more than four inches by twelve right at the ground. It must belong to the basement they had mentioned. Someone had said something about a window, but it wasn't on the drawing they studied.

Obviously too small for a person to get through, but he could throw a grenade in there. Quickly, he whispered that information on his radio to the Special Agent in Charge.

"If we go in, I'll have you put one in there as well as the ones we lob through the front," his commander told him. Special Agent Four acknowledged the order into the voice-activated mike on his shoulder and crouched down to wait.

* * * * * * * * * * * * * * * * * * *

The most difficult positions to attain were those of the two Safety team members who were assigned the front porch. One at a time, they slithered across the front walkway and rolled underneath the porch. There wasn't enough room to kneel so they lay on their sides, their legs tensed to spring into action. They didn't want to be completely under the porch, but they had to be under the overhang enough to be invisible if one of the suspects should come out again. They wriggled into position, their weapons digging into them in the crowded quarters. Silently, they waited — listening to each other's breathing — waiting for the action to start.

* * * * * * * * * * * * * * * * * *

It was beginning to rain — rain in earnest. Pete pulled the hood of his sweatshirt up over his head and shivered slightly. Sgt. Fisher looked at him but didn't say anything. Now was not the time to worry about anyone's comfort. The two of them crouched behind the pile of mossy logs on the ground. Pete held his two-meter transceiver to his ear, hoping to hear Kim. Sgt. Fisher held his two-way radio tightly to his ear, monitoring for any instructions from the SWAT team.

Pete had overheard a few of Sgt. Fisher's instructions on the radio. In his mind, he saw all of the armed men posted around the cabin. Ten armed men outside and two armed men inside and one girl — a girl named Kim who had suddenly become very important to him.

* * * * * * * * * * * * * * * * * *

Marc couldn't stand it any longer.

"Pete?" he said quietly into his microphone. "Anything happening?"

"No," Pete replied in a whisper. "They've got the place surrounded. Now they're just waiting."

Marc buried his face in his hands and took a deep breath. Lt. Keller, who had returned to the base cabin after escorting the team to the location, came over and put a hand on Marc's shoulder.

"Trust them, son. They're the best we have."

"I just hope the best is good enough," Marc said solemnly.

Chapter 21

Bernie

In the Cabin
6:45 p.m.

"Okay, let's go over it one more time — you keep to the side of the road — in the trees, if possible. If any cars come along the road, hide in the brush somewhere — can't take any chances."

"All right, all right!" Bernie shouted. "What do you think I am, anyway? — your little kid? You know how many cars I've ripped off in my life? And now you're trying to tell me how to do it. You think I don't know enough not to let people see me?"

The two men glared at each other. Kim sat beside Willy's couch, bathing his face and watching the scene before her. Bernie walked over to the woodstove, opened the door, and defiantly lit a cigarette from the flame inside. For once, Joe didn't tell him to go outside to smoke. Bernie leaned back against the wall by the woodstove and blew smoke rings toward the ceiling, watching them with a glint of amusement in his eyes. Joe ignored him.

"Hey, Sheila — look at this one," Bernie said, reaching out and poking her chair with his foot.

"What?" She woke up with a start.

"I said look at this!"

He blew a giant smoke ring that wafted upward and then blended with the dingy boards of the ceiling. Sheila didn't say anything for a minute — just sat there, cradling her injured arm.

"I'm hungry, Joe," she whined. "What's there to eat?"

"I don't know — ask *her*," he replied, gesturing over his shoulder at Kim.

"Hey girl. You got any more of those fancy potato chips left?"

Silently, Kim got up and went to the kitchen. The minute she was out of view of the men, she put her hand into her pocket and sent a quick message to Pete and Marc — "Bernie coming out soon," she sent rapidly in Morse code.

"Hey, whatcha doing — growing the potatoes?" came Sheila's impatient demand.

Kim grabbed the last bag of barbecue-flavored potato chips from the shelf and carried them over and plopped them in Sheila's lap and then went back to Willy.

She watched as Sheila struggled to open the bag with one hand. Kim wasn't about to help her unless Sheila ordered her to. The wounded woman wrestled with the bag and finally grabbed the bag with her teeth and ripped it open. Bernie's big hand plunged into the bag before Sheila could even get one.

"Hey, you big ape — aren't you supposed to be out stealing a car or something?" Sheila snapped.

"That's me — on my way," Bernie laughed. "I think you might live after all, Sheila — you've got your normal sweet temper back." Turning to Joe, he said, "I'll be back in an hour tops — make sure everything's taken care of."

His eyes flickered briefly toward Kim, and Joe nodded. He slammed the door behind him, and they heard him go whistling across the porch.

"Stupid idiot," Joe growled. "I hope he doesn't whistle while he's stealing the car."

Willy started coughing just then — huge paroxysms of coughing that left him gasping and slightly blue.

"Let me fix the tent again," Kim suggested. She got up quickly and moved to the kitchen to put the water on to boil.

She came back into the living room carrying a rusted pan she'd found under the sink.

"I'm going to put this one on the woodstove just to keep some extra water hot," she explained.

"Good," said Sheila. "I'd like to try soaking my arm again — that made it feel better."

Joe didn't look up. He was busy unloading and reloading one of the two guns.

* * * * * * * * * * * * * * * * * * *

The minute Kim had sent the signal that Bernie was coming out soon, Pete relayed the message to Sgt. Fisher who in turn contacted the SWAT team. There was a brief movement by the edge of the front porch as the two Safety team members pulled themselves completely out of view under the overhang.

They needn't have worried. Still whistling and smoking, Bernie jumped over the broken boards and down on to the gravel below. Without looking back, he set off down the rutted driveway that led over the incline to the road.

One of the safety team, peering out from under the porch, noticed that Bernie was scratching his leg as he walked.

* * * * * * * * * * * * * * * * * * *

"One and two, go after him. Let him get far enough from the house and then take him down — hold him — we'll want to question him." The Special Agent in Charge gave the terse orders into his hand-held radio as Bernie walked jauntily toward the road.

* * * * * * * * * * * * * * * * * * *

At last it was coming to an end, Bernie thought gratefully. Getting the car would be a cinch. Even if the people had decided to retrieve their keys, he could hot wire it in a flash. By the time he got back to the cabin with it, that stupid girl would be dead, and they would be on their way. He smiled a little thinking of Kim. He would have liked to be the one to "take care of her," but it seemed like Joe was giving the orders these days.

He was sure Willy would die before the night was over, but there was no convincing Joe to leave him behind. In a grudging kind of way, he admired Joe's loyalty to his brother.

So let the kid die, and they could dump him off somewhere and continue on. Just him and Joe and Sheila. Sheila was a nuisance but she didn't really harm anyone. Besides, it was fun to torment her.

Once they crossed into California, he was sure Joe would be willing to do a couple of jobs. And then, when the time was right, Bernie planned to take a gun and the money and head east. And if Joe and Sheila got in the way . . . well, that was their tough luck. He had no desire to go to Mexico.

* * * * * * * * * * * * * * * * * *

Like black cats stalking their prey, the two agents kept to either side of Bernie as he approached the main road. They couldn't risk letting him get out of their sight for even a second or the darkness would swallow him up. But they also had to let him get far enough from the house that if their struggle made any noise, it wouldn't alert the other suspects in the cabin.

The girl had said he was unarmed. It was hard to tell in the dark, but he didn't appear to have any telltale bulges of a weapon under his jacket. He had stopped whistling and was starting to move cautiously himself as he approached the road. Silently, the two men closed in from the sides.

* * * * * * * * * * * * * * * * * *

Bernie never heard his assailants. At the same moment that the booted foot of one man kicked his knee forward, a strong hand cupped over his mouth and slammed him backward to the ground. The wind was already knocked out of him, but a black figure dropped a knee to Bernie's diaphragm. He lay there motionless, his breathing paralyzed — his body sending frantic pain messages to his brain.

Roughly, the two men in black rolled him on his stomach. One handcuffed him while the other slapped three-inch-wide tape across his mouth. Then a black hood was jerked into place over his head. Bernie struggled frantically for a moment and then quivered silently on the ground — disoriented, sightless, silenced, and breathless — the fight was gone out of him.

As they half led, half dragged him along the edge of the road, thoughts jumbled through his brain. Police! They were obviously some kind of police — silent police. Then one of them spoke quickly into a radio, announcing his capture. There was a brief acknowledgment. In seconds, Bernie heard the sound of a car approaching. The door opened and a man got out. Bernie heard him speak briefly to his two captors and then their retreating footsteps which quickly merged with the black silence of the night.

This new man grabbed his arm and shoved him roughly through the doorway of what appeared to be a van. Then the man pushed him down on a metal bench and told the driver something about going back to the base cabin.

* * * * * * * * * * * * * * * * * * *

Bernie struggled against the hood and the tape. It was hard to breathe and his back still felt as if someone had stuck a pick axe through it. He moved in his seat, trying to get a deep breath.

"Just hold still," Sgt. Fisher advised him.

Bernie held still.

* * * * * * * * * * * * * * * * * * *

"They got him," Pete told Marc on two meters. "I think they're bringing him to your cabin for interrogation. The scene here seems quiet — everyone has gone back into position."

Marc acknowledged the call. The same information was being transmitted by the Special Agent in Charge to Lt. Keller. They were bringing the suspect here. Once again, Marc felt his own anger rise up within him. What he would like to do to that guy!

He heard the crunch of gravel outside and then Sgt. Fisher and a SWAT team member appeared in the doorway, shoving Bernie ahead of them.

Marc looked up at the tall hooded man, half struggling as Sgt. Fisher and the van driver wrestled him into a chair.

"Ready?" Sgt. Fisher said to Lt. Keller.

"Ready." Lt. Keller answered.

Sgt. Fisher reached over and jerked the black hood over the top of the prisoner's head. Bernie blinked furiously in the bright light. While he was still trying to adjust his eyes, Sgt. Fisher grabbed the edge of the tape on his mouth and ripped it loose.

The adhesive caught at Bernie's several days' growth of beard. He howled and cursed in protest. For a moment, he tried to fight his way to his feet, but three officers jammed him back in the chair.

Marc stared hard at the man, and Bernie, feeling the intensity of his gaze, returned it. A cold chill swept through Marc as the steely ice blue eyes penetrated the space between them.

Chapter 22

Questions

Base Cabin
7:30 p.m.

"**T**his is him," Sgt. Fisher said, handing Lt. Keller an FBI want sheet with Bernie Knissen's photo and record on it. Lt. Keller looked over the long list of robbery convictions and whistled. Bernie Knissen had committed seventeen robberies before he was convicted the first time. Obviously, prison had done nothing to reform him — he now had a string of six more to add to the list. He glanced at the sullen suspect who had been shackled to a chair in the corner. Sgt. Fisher had already read him his rights. After his initial stare at Marc, Bernie hadn't even looked up once — just directed his eyes toward the floor until the sergeant told him he was being arrested on suspicion of bank robbery, kidnapping, and murder.

"Murder?" he said in surprise. "I never killed anybody!"

"Remember that guard you hit in the hospital," said Lt. Blaine who had been watching the proceedings silently. "Well, he died. He was one of my best men," he added.

Bernie shrugged his shoulders.

"You guys must be thinking of someone else. I'm just here on a fishing trip."

"Okay, Bernie, we've got some questions for you and we want some answers. Who else was in that cabin with you and what are they planning to do?" Lt. Keller asked

Silence.

"Bernie, the cabin's surrounded. We've got a team ready to go in there any minute — your friends could all be killed," Lt. Blaine added.

Bernie shrugged again. He looked up and smiled.

"What makes you think they're my friends?" he said quietly.

Lt. Keller sighed and tried a different tack.

"Why don't you have a gun, Bernie?"

Bernie smiled. "A gun!" he exclaimed in mock horror. "What would I need a gun for? I was just walking down the road to enjoy the moonlight—besides, I don't even own a gun."

"There's no moon tonight, Bernie, and we know you were on your way out to steal a car."

Bernie's eyes opened wide with shock. For a minute, he didn't say anything — just stared at each person in the room with hatred.

"We also know that one of the men in the cabin is seriously wounded and that Kim is taking care of him," Lt. Keller continued.

"Kim? You mean the little nursie?" Bernie snorted with laughter. "Man, she's history by now."

Marc flew to his feet and came across the room. Sgt. Fisher caught him by the arm.

"Hold on, Marc — he's just having a good time — don't let him get your goat."

Bernie looked up and saw the anger and worry on Marc's face. He smiled wickedly.

"Oh, are you the little nursie's boyfriend?"

"What have you done to her?" Marc heard himself shout.

"Wouldn't you like to know?" Bernie laughed. "One thing, I guarantee — you'll never see her again."

Marc turned frantically to Sgt. Fisher.

"Do something — do something *now*," he insisted.

Sgt. Fisher forced Marc back across the room and pushed him gently into a chair.

"Just relax, son," the sergeant told him. "He's playing to an audience — there's no reason to believe anything he says. We'll get him out of here in a minute, but Lt. Keller wanted to question him before booking him in jail."

Marc felt hysteria rising in him.

"If they've hurt her," he said fiercely, "I'm going to break every bone in that guy's body."

Sgt. Fisher put both hands on Marc's shoulders and looked him squarely in the eyes.

"No, you're not," he said quietly. "Because you're not like him. I know all about you, Marc — you're highly respected for the courage and resourcefulness you showed last summer in the wilderness. Now, Marc, we need you here as a radio operator, but if you can't do it, we'll take you back to the station."

Marc drew a deep breath and unclenched his fists.

"I can do it," he said.

He got up and sat down heavily at the seat in front of the two-meter gear. He tried not to look at Bernie again, but the insistent questions of Lt. Keller were like buzz saws in his brain.

"Who's in there with you? How many weapons? Where is the girl?"

Then when there was no answer, Lt. Keller started reading a list of the prior convictions and charges against Bernie.

Bernie was thinking. Thinking harder than he had ever thought before in his life. It was over. They knew who he was. The news that the hospital guard had died meant that there was now a murder rap hanging over his head. And the girl was surely dead by now, too. He would be an accomplice in that murder — he most likely would get the death penalty.

Suddenly, Morse code started coming in over Marc's transceiver. Marc grabbed a pencil to copy, and the room silenced.

"Joe has two handguns. Will try to come out soon. Wait for 'O'."

Marc translated quickly for Lt. Keller.

"She's not dead," he exclaimed and looked triumphantly over at Bernie who appeared totally surprised.

"You mean Nursie has been sending you guys code?" Bernie said incredulously. The sentence that was already formed in his brain, ready to come out was, *Man Joe should have shot her the first night like I told him.* But he never said it. Instead, Bernie paused and said something he had never

179

said to a police officer in his life — "Let me help you save her life!"

He began to talk frantically, half begging, half promising.

"Joe's going to kill her any minute. Take me back there — I can talk him out of it. I know I can!"

The men didn't seem interested in his requests. Instead, they asked him for specifics about weapons and ammunition and the layout of the cabin. Bernie answered them off-handedly but then returned to his plea for them to take him back to bargain with Joe.

After a few more minutes of this, Lt. Keller and Sgt. Fisher grabbed the suspect by both arms and jerked him to his feet.

"You've said enough — I think it's time for you to go to jail," Lt. Keller said as two uniformed deputies came forward to take the man to a waiting patrol car.

As Bernie was escorted forcibly to the door, he looked over at Marc.

"Your girlfriend doesn't have a chance unless you let me help. She'll be dead soon. I guarantee it!"

He spat on the floor as the two officers dragged him through the doorway.

Marc listened intently as Lt. Keller and Lt. Blaine discussed the situation with each other and then on the radio with the SWAT team commander.

"The suspect has indicated the girl's going to be killed. I think we should go in now." Lt. Keller said.

"Just a minute," the commander replied. In a second, he came back on. "I'm here with the other radio operator — he's told me again that the girl said she's going to try to come out soon. Let's give her a few more minutes and then move."

"Roger," said Lt. Keller. "I have all your backups in place."

Lt. Keller switched to another radio and talked quickly to the fire engine and medics staged under cover down the road. In the case of a fire fight, their services might be needed and needed quickly.

Marc stood up and paced back and forth, looking at his watch every few seconds. Subconsciously, he noted that the repeaters had grown quiet too. Kim's transmission on simplex was probably being heard within a five to ten mile radius. He visualized the ham community glued to their radios as this life and death drama unfolded.

Chapter 23

O — — — — Means Out!

Hostage Cabin
7:45 p.m.

The cabin was almost dark except for the glow from the woodstove. Sheila sat by the fire's warmth, rubbing her arm gently and humming a tune Kim had never heard. Kim had just completed re-installing Willy's steam tent. She folded the cloth back so that it was half draped around his head. The sound of his strained breathing filled the room, and Kim felt her own lungs ache sympathetically with his battle. She stood up and took the empty kettle to the kitchen to reheat.

The pan on the woodstove was boiling. Kim went over to move the rusty pan to the back of the woodstove where it could stay at a simmer until needed. As she walked by Joe, he reached out and caught her hand.

"Give me your watch," he said gruffly, catching the flexible metal band and jerking it down over her fingers.

Kim pulled her hand back. She started to protest but the fierce look in his eyes stopped her. Warily, she edged her way to the woodstove, her left hand in her pocket, furtively turning her radio on. Sheila watched her like a hawk.

"Don't get near me — I don't think it's going to be healthy to be around you, pretty soon," Sheila warned, looking over at Joe knowingly. "Isn't it time yet?" she asked. "Bernie ought to be back any minute."

Kim heard her heart thudding at these veiled exchanges. What were they talking about? She watched in horror as Joe laid one of the pistols across his leg and glanced again at Kim's watch. Suddenly, Sheila sprang to her feet.

"What's that?" she demanded. "I hear something outside."

183

"Oh, probably just a raccoon or skunk passing by," Joe said.

"No!" Sheila insisted. "It sounded like footsteps! I bet the girl signaled someone!"

"Now how could she do that?" Joe said patiently. Then a slow look of remembering crossed his face.

"Hey, when we were in that grocery store, I saw a newspaper headline that said something about girl Amateur Radio operator kidnapped!" His voice rose to a crescendo of accusation as he bolted across the room and slammed Kim back against the wall next to the woodstove. "Have you got some sort of radio?" he yelled right in her face, one hand around her neck.

"No, no, please, don't," Kim begged as he pulled the loaded gun up and aimed it at her head.

Then the world changed to slow motion. Kim heard a loud pounding in her ears and through it came a terrible cough and then a weak voice that said, "Joe, help me, Joe."

For a split second, Joe turned his head toward Willy.

Kim's right hand reached behind her for the pan of water on the woodstove at the same time that her left hand plunged into her pocket to grab her two-meter rig. As if in a trance, she saw her arm come up with the pan and the scalding liquid dash onto Joe's chest. In a howl of rage, he loosened his hands from her and grabbed frantically at his scalded flesh.

* * * * * * * * * * * * * * * * * *

Pete need not have worried about his ability to pass information quickly. When Kim sent "O", he shouted "Out" to the Special Agent in Charge next to him. The message was relayed instantly to the men.

* * * * * * * * * * * * * * * * * *

There was no memory of the door opening, but Kim knew she must have done it. Her feet pounded across the porch and as she saw the hole left by the broken boards, she leaped over

it, dimly hoping that she wouldn't break an ankle when she landed on the ground below the porch.

Her running stride hit the ground and as she took the first steps toward the forest, added terror gripped her as strong hands connected to hulking black figures grabbed her out of nowhere. Horrible fear mixed with a strange flying sensation as they zoomed with her toward the woods. Somehow Bernie must have come back for her!

They were saying something to her, but her conscious brain didn't register their words — "You're okay, you're okay — RUN! RUN!"

She heard the blur of their voices and at the same time sensed a huge beam of light behind her and the sound of a door slamming shut.

Then a horrible thud as she was slammed face down into the wet soil with such force that the wind was knocked out of her. The heavy black figures dropped heavily on top of her too, and Kim felt her deflated lungs struggle for air between their weight and hard coldness of the forest floor. Her young body fought to breathe, and an energy she had never felt before gave her one last burst to try and fight against her attackers. One of them had his hand over her mouth so she couldn't scream. Everything was getting hazy — there was a voice in her ear, but she couldn't understand it.

Then the voice got louder. Dimly, she realized that she could breathe again — although painfully — and that the hands that were holding her down were not hurting her.

"Kim!" the voice said insistently. "Kim! We're with the Sheriff's office — lie still. We don't want you to get shot!"

They must have known how hard it was for her to comprehend their message, so the voice kept repeating it over and over coupled, with "You're okay, now — you're safe."

She turned her head and saw kind eyes staring at her beneath the brim of a black baseball cap.

"Come on," the man said. "We have to get further back."

She looked at them in a daze. The idea of moving her legs to stand up seemed completely foreign to her, but they picked her up between them and ran through the woods. As they left the edge of the trees, Kim turned her head to see a huge beam of light aimed at the cabin door. Its brilliance lit up the area like daylight. A loud voice was talking on a bullhorn.

"This is the FBI. Throw down your gun!"

"Two guns," Kim said faintly, as the men stopped with her and leaned her up against a tree. "He has two guns."

"What kind of guns?"

"Handguns."

"What are the suspect's names?

"Joe's the only one you have to worry about. Sheila is wounded and Willy is dying."

Quickly, the information was radioed back to the SWAT team and Kim heard the message on the bullhorn change to

"Joe! This is the FBI. Throw out both your guns and come out with your hands up. We have Bernie in custody. Come out now so we can help your brother."

She waited fearfully for gunfire, thinking of Willy lying there helpless on the couch. Silence.

"Come on," one of the men said gently. "Let's get you of here. Can you walk?"

"I don't know," Kim said.

Her legs felt like rubber as she took a tentative step away from the tree. Two strong arms encircled her and she gratefully leaned on the men as they half-carried her back to the road. An ambulance was waiting at the edge of the trees. Three medics got out of the cab.

"If she's okay, we need to take the ambulance over for backup," one of them said.

"I'm okay," Kim said weakly.

She focused her eyes on a name tag that read "John Hendricks E.M.T." attached to one of the men kneeling beside her. He and another medic helped her over to sit down in the back seat of a patrol car that had just pulled up. The other two medics got back in the ambulance and drove slowly down the road toward the cabin.

One of the men in black touched her shoulder.

"Sorry we had to be so rough, but we had to get you out of there," he said.

"I'm not complaining," Kim said, starting to smile a little.

The two men raised their hands in sort of a half wave and then disappeared back into the forest blackness. Kim stared after them, trying to comprehend the events of the last few minutes.

John Hendricks had a big kit with him, but he didn't open it.

"How are you feeling?" he asked Kim.

"Scared," she said, feeling her lips tremble as she spoke.

"Anything hurt?" he asked, gently patting her trousered legs.

"No," she said, shaking her head. "For a minute when I fell down, I couldn't breathe, but I think I'm okay now."

The medic talked to her for awhile. Someone put a coat around her. She had started to shake all over — so hard that her teeth were chattering. An officer got a blanket from the trunk of the car and wrapped her in it. Gradually, her trembling ceased.

* * * * * * * * * * * * * * * * * *

One hand clutching his burning chest and stomach, and the other holding his gun ready to fire, Joe had rushed to the door behind Kim. Fury surged through him — she would not escape!

He crashed his shoulder against the partially opened door and then reeled backward as a paralyzing beam of light caught him in the doorway. Frantically, he slammed the door shut and ran back to the living room.

"They're out there!" he yelled to Sheila.

Whimpering, she cowered in her chair, pulling the sleeping bag up around her as if to block out the world.

Willy coughed softly, too weak to bring enough air in to make much noise.

"It's over," Joe said to Sheila. "That's it."

"This is the FBI," a voice was blaring again. "Come out with your hands on top of your head."

"Shoot them!" Sheila said, rousing from her huddle. "Come on, Joe, shoot them!"

Joe grabbed her uninjured arm and propelled her toward the door, half crazed with pain himself.

"I'm sorry, Baby, I'm sure sorry," he said.

* * * * * * * * * * * * * * * * *

The wailing howl of the ambulance startled Kim as it came roaring down the road with its lights blazing and horn blaring. The fire engine lumbered after it and then finally another patrol car. Kim thought she caught a brief glimpse of Joe in the backseat but she wasn't sure.

"They just surrendered," a sheriff's officer told her. "Nobody got hurt — everything's okay."

"The guy named Willy," Kim said softly. "I don't think he's as bad as the others. In a way, he saved my life. If he hadn't called out to Joe when he did . . ." she shuddered and left the sentence unfinished.

* * * * * * * * * * * * * * * * *

They were driving down the road now. Kim sat in the back seat next to a sheriff's officer. Her shaking had stopped, but she could still feel her heart thudding away rapidly. A terrible fatigue was washing over her.

"Where are we going?" she asked. "Where's Marc?"

"Right here," the officer driving said as they pulled off the road onto a gravel driveway that led to a well-lit cabin in a grove of trees.

The minute their car turned in, the front door of the cabin was flung open, and Marc came running out. Kim reached for the car door handle, but he already had it open. "Are you okay?" he asked looking at her mud-streaked face.

She nodded. Suddenly, she felt an avalanche of tears welling up in her eyes. Marc pulled her gently from the car and enfolded her in his arms. She closed her eyes and for the first time in three days she felt safe.

Now he was leading her into the cabin. Kim squinted as her eyes adjusted to the bright lights. The cabin was full of uniformed officers. They were all smiling at her and chatting happily among themselves. She noticed a tall distinguished silver-haired man standing by the door. He was wearing blue jeans and a sweatshirt and was staring right at her. When he saw Kim return his glance, he walked over.

"I bet you're Pete," said Kim.

"KH6XM at your service," he said smiling and taking Kim's hand in both of his. "Glad to meet you KA7SJP."

Then he bent over and kissed Kim on the cheek, and she returned it with a bear hug of her own.

* * * * * * * * * * * * * * * * * *

The party atmosphere in the cabin might have gone on forever, but there were things to do. After Kim had been given a chance to wash up and a steaming cup of hot chocolate, she sat by the fire until she was warm. Lt. Keller told her they needed her to go to the Newport Sheriff's office and sign statements against her abductors.

"Has anyone called my parents?" she asked anxiously.

"Yes," said Marc. "I did that the minute I heard you were safe. I gave the message to a ham in Waldport, and she called your parents. They said to tell you they love you, and they can hardly wait for us to get there. I'm going to drive you home as soon as the officers are done debriefing you."

* * * * * * * * * * * * * * * * * *

Newport Sheriff's Office
10 p.m.

It was another hour before Kim completed all the paperwork that would indict the Willamette Valley Gang of kidnapping and attempted murder. That, added to the charges already filed by the FBI of robbery and murder, should be enough to put them away for quite awhile, Lt. Keller told her.

John Alsance, AA6BC, ARES Coordinator for the Mid Coastal Region was also there at the sheriff's office to greet them warmly.

"My shift is over, and I had intended to go back to Salem for a couple of days anyway to visit my brother. Why don't you let me drive you both home in your car? You both look exhausted. My brother can bring me back." Kim and Marc readily agreed to the offer. They climbed in the back seat of John's car.

"I have so much to tell you," Kim said as they drove through the darkness toward Corvallis and Salem.

"I'm listening," Marc responded, putting his arm around her.

Kim started to tell the story of her ordeal, but somehow it seemed too overwhelming to relate just now. She put her head on Marc's shoulder and closed her eyes. Soon, she was fast asleep, and in a few minutes, Marc was too. John turned and looked at the tired young couple and smiled.

Chapter 24

Merry Christmas

The Stafford House
December 28th, 6 p.m.

T he group at the table applauded as Kim entered the dining room. "It's about time," her brother Brandon said. "How can you sleep all day after an adventure like that? I want to hear all about it — did the crooks have machine guns or what?"

Kim laughed, yawned, and then laughed again. She glanced at her watch which Lt. Keller had retrieved from Joe and given back to her. Six o'clock! Indeed she must have slept all day. She had just gotten up a half hour ago and showered. The wonderful aroma of turkey and dressing baking had reached her even upstairs, and now she felt her stomach rumbling.

She looked around the table and felt tears come to her eyes at the sight of her parents, Brandon, Marc, his parents, her Uncle Steve, W6RHM, who had managed to fly up for the celebration, and Pete Sheffield, KH6XM, looking delighted to be included in this family gathering. A tremendous feeling of love and gratitude swept over her as she realized how much all of these people meant to her.

Always the one for breaking an emotional moment, Brandon spoke up. "Let's eat! " he said.

"But first," interrupted Mr. Stafford, "let's give thanks."

The group held hands while Kim's father gave a heartfelt prayer of thanksgiving. Then there was happy chatter and tons of food: turkey, dressing, sweet potatoes, peas and water chestnuts, cranberry sauce, fresh baked rolls, Waldorf salad, and rich pumpkin and pecan pies.

"What did you do, Mom — save the whole dinner for me?"

"That's exactly what she did," Kim's father said.

"Yeah, I tried to get her to make it on Christmas, but she just wouldn't," said Brandon teasing.

"Oh you!" Kim laughed, reaching out to punch him.

They ate and talked and ate some more. Midway through the dinner, Lt. Blaine from Portland called and asked for Kim.

"You seemed concerned about Willy," he said. "I thought you'd like to know that he's in critical but stable condition. He was airlifted to a trauma center here in Portland. No one's predicting whether he'll pull through or not, but he seems to have a chance. Bernie and Joe are in the Multnomah County Jail and Sheila will be there as soon as her arm's okay. She spent the night in the hospital under guard. From what I hear, she's giving everyone a rough time."

Kim laughed. "I don't doubt that."

They talked for a few minutes and Kim asked about trial dates. She obviously was going to be needed as a witness.

Kim went back to the table and briefly told what Lt. Blaine had said. She could tell from the looks on all of their faces that they were eager for more information. No one asked about the details of her horrible imprisonment, but it was obvious that they wanted to hear the story. So after dinner, they went in the living room, and Kim told the story from start to finish — beginning with the hospital Christmas party and ending with her flight out the cabin door.

"I had no idea there would be SWAT team men there — in fact, I've never seen one. When those guys in black grabbed me, I somehow thought it was Bernie and maybe a friend of his. You can't imagine how scared I was."

Brandon shook his head. "Gee, Sis, you should have just punched the bank robbers out — like this!"

He got to his feet and shadow-boxed invisible foes across the living room. Pete laughed and grabbed him and pulled him down on the couch beside him.

They talked for another hour or so. Everyone had questions, and at times Kim found it very difficult to relive the painful events of the preceding days. Her father was watching her, and finally he said, "Okay, that's enough for now. We've forgotten something very important."

"What?" Brandon asked.

"Kim hasn't opened her presents."

"Well, neither have we!" declared Brandon.

So there was more laughter as Brandon brought a stack of brightly wrapped presents from under the tree and piled them on the floor. Brandon ripped into his happily while Kim and her parents seemed more content to just sit and watch.

"I think I'd rather wait until tomorrow to do this," Kim said.

"Well there is one you have to see," Marc said. "I hope you'll forgive me — but I opened it for you."

"You what?" Kim said. "You mean while I was being kidnapped and everyone was worrying about me, you were opening my presents?" She knew that wasn't true, but it was fun to tease Marc.

"Come on," he said, taking her hand. "I'll show you."

They went up the stairs to her bedroom with Brandon trailing along behind.

"Look!" Marc said, pointing to the packet setup next to her computer.

"Oh!" Kim gasped, unbelieving.

"It's from your parents — they told me to go ahead and set it up when they found out that packet could be used to help track you down."

Kim sat down at the computer and stared at the new equipment with awe.

"Go ahead, turn it on," Marc urged.

She flipped the computer switch on. Where there had formerly been just eight items on the master menu, now there was a ninth — packet. Kim put the indicator arrow by packet and punched Enter. A screen came up telling her how to access the Salem node. She had worked with packet before at the university Amateur station, so she quickly accessed the node.

"Why don't you bring up the local bulletin board?" Marc suggested.

"Why, I'm not on it, yet, am I?" and then seeing Marc's wide grin, she punched in "C WA7SHP"

The screen flashed a greeting.

"Hello Kim, Welcome to WA7SHP's MSYS BBS in Turner, OR. You have unread mail."

"Type R M for read mine," Marc said.

Kim rapidly typed the command and then waited while the message came up.

"December 25th 1 a.m. Merry Christmas Kim! 88's Marc."

"88's!" Brandon said in disgust behind them. "That means love and kisses — oh no, more mushy stuff."

"But, but," stammered Kim. "If you wrote that on Christmas, how did you know I'd ever get back alive to read it?"

"I just knew," Marc said softly.

Then he took her face in both of his hands and kissed her gently. Kim looked up at Brandon watching from the doorway.

"Go away, Brandon," she said.

Author's Note

Like Kim, I was a Candystriper, and later, an adult hospital volunteer. One time as I was delivering flowers and mail to patients, I saw a guard posted outside a hospital room.

"Why is he there?" I asked a nurse.

"Because the guy inside is a member of a gang and was attacked by another gang. We're afraid that his friends may try to rescue him or that his enemies may try to finish the job."

Needless to say, I gave that hall a wide berth on the rest of my errands. Kim wasn't so lucky.

I had a lot of fun writing this story, and I also had many willing helpers. First, I would like to thank Captain Leon Riggs of Marion County Sheriff's Department for walking me step by step through a SWAT team rescue. My many conversations with him have given me new appreciation for the fine and difficult work that agencies like his perform.

And thanks to April Moell, WA6OPS, and Joe Moell, KØOV, for their help with the hospital and "North Pole Network" scenes. Their tireless volunteer efforts have cheered many children at Christmas.

Thanks to Fred Molesworth, AF7S, for all of his technical suggestions, and to Hollie Molesworth, KA7SJP, for once again lending her call to Kim.

Willy wants to thank Sharon Gooley, R.N. for her first aid suggestions to Kim. It was Kim's and Sharon's efforts which kept Willy alive.

Heartfelt thanks to my aunt, Sidney Dawson, for her hours of proofreading and her constant support and encouragement. And to my brother, Steve Jensen, W6RHM, Kim wants to say thank you for his suggestion of the "J" antenna and all of his other technical expertise.

Special thanks to my stepmother, Lenore Jensen, W6NAZ, who is truly a "high class" Amateur Radio operator. Her

198

suggestions have been invaluable. And thanks to my family: my husband, Dave, son, Michael, KA7ITR, and son, Bob, for their encouragement and patience. I guess I should thank our cat, Bandon, too, as her frequent scampers across the computer keyboard while I was working may have added substantially to the plot.

To all of the Salem-Keizer School students who have enthusiastically praised Night Signals, I want to add a special thanks. I have enjoyed speaking in your schools this year and telling you about Amateur Radio. It's a wonderful hobby, and I look forward to meeting many new friends on the air in the coming years.

73,

Cynthia Wall, KA7ITT

Cynthia Wall, KA7ITT

To Learn More About Amateur Radio . . .

You and your friends can be part of the excitement of Amateur Radio, just like Kim and Marc! Join the thousands of people who love to talk over the air and meet new friends around the world. Write to us and ask for a free information package that tells you how easy it is to get your ham radio license and join in the fun and adventures:

ARRL
Department H
225 Main Street
Newington, CT 06111

Morse Code Characters

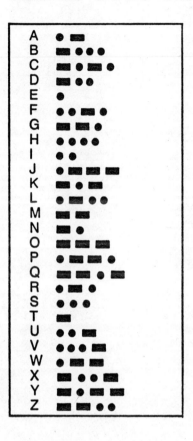

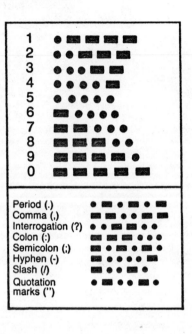